THE SEVENTH SHRINE

ORLAND BISHOP

the Seventh Shrine

MEDITATIONS ON THE AFRICAN SPIRITUAL JOURNEY

From the Middle Passage to the Mountaintop

Lindisfarne Books | 2017

2017
Lindisfarne Books
An imprint of SteinerBooks / Anthroposophic Press, Inc.
610 Main St., Great Barrington, MA 01230
www.steinerbooks.org

COVER IMAGE: Joseph Mallord William Turner (1775–1851): *Slave Ship (Slavers Throwing Overboard the Dead and Dying—Typhoon Coming On)*, 1840, Museum of Fine Arts, Boston
DESIGN: Jens Jensen

William Turner exhibited this painting with his unfinished long poem *Fallacies of Hope:*

Aloft all hands, strike the top-masts and belay;
Yon angry setting sun and fierce-edged clouds
Declare the Typhon's coming.
Before it sweeps your decks, throw overboard
The dead and dying—ne'er heed their chains
Hope, Hope, fallacious Hope!
Where is thy market now?

LIBRARY OF CONGRESS CONTROL NUMBER: 2016963559

ISBN: 978-1-58420-964-5 (paperback)
ISBN: 978-1-58420-965-2 (eBook)

CONTENTS

The Negro Speaks of Rivers

I've known rivers:
I've known rivers ancient as the world and older
than the flow of human blood in human veins.

My soul has grown deep like the rivers.

I bathed in the Euphrates when dawns were young.
I built my hut near the Congo and it lulled me to sleep.
I looked upon the Nile and raised the pyramids above it.
I heard the singing of the Mississippi when Abe Lincoln
went down to New Orleans, and I've seen its muddy
bosom turn all golden in the sunset.

I've known rivers:
Ancient, dusky rivers.

My soul has grown deep like the rivers.

—Langston Hughes

INTRODUCTION

This book tells the story of the path my soul is taking—of the places, the processes, and the people that have inspired its awakening. It tells of the timeless currents that flow from the ancestral world into my own expression of life. It reveals my challenges in crossing the boundaries of my soul into the world where the agreements of my life can unfold.

My development unfolded through the social impulses of certain vital places: Guyana, Brooklyn, New York; Los Angeles; and South and West Africa.

Within these social spaces the relationships are cultivated. These relationships further provided the context for the forming of my own identity. Friends, mentors, teachers, and colleagues with whom I explore the meaning of life have shaped my aspirations. I chose to learn and do as work in the world.

Various processes have supported the unfolding of my soul potential, from my academic education to mentorship. I have come to understand that the highest prerogative of the soul is initiation. These processes have given me different levels of access to my inner life and my outer understanding of the world. They continue to shape how I live. They shape with whom I create my agreements. I explore in this book events of my life that reveal the relationship directly to the ancestral world. This relationship serves as the purpose for my work. I share how I was guided into conscious initiation.

We know the soul to be as ancient as the world. It lives in a stream of memory, often referred to as the ancestral world. Through the soul, our personal and collective dreams, and often prophecies, are transmitted. It is the stream into which we are born and out of which we live. It is the source of our individual striving—of the communities we form and of civilizations we create. Through the soul, we draw on ancestral memory to connect us to events before our birth and to divine the possibilities within our futures.

When I navigate the currents of the soul, I find myself within my ancestral pool. I find myself swimming in their grief, and the longing during the great event and initiation called the Middle Passage. I find myself in their collective soul journey from a place of homeland to a dream of the Promised Land. This book is a telling of the soul striving of people of African heritage into the American experience of creating a community—a community created for the possibilities of new covenants within the larger collective sphere of human life.

The work to which I have dedicated my life is to attend to the ancestral shrines. Ancestral shrines are co-creative imaginative influences on how I see the world. They serve to enhance the human encounters that form relationships and communities within which I work and live. The primary emphasis of my work is to support the recovery of the individual's capacity to stand in openness for the higher purpose of one's own life. My work is in service to the creative freedom of others. It is to communicate on a level where agreements are possible. It is to reveal the possibilities of a shared future.

It takes a form of mentorship. Mentorship is the guiding of a youthful impulse to the thresholds of initiation and the creating of community that prepares for their return. In the larger sense, the work endeavors to shape a collective holding of the cultural task of creating a compassionate economy to support human development, ecological sustainability, and the deeper covenants of the heart.

The book reveals through the spiritual tradition of African Gnosis my identification with the impulses of particular individuals in the history of the African experience in America. Their lives and work reveal the spiritual frameworks that have guided me to my understanding of the promise of the Spirit of America.

The book navigates the flow of the American stream from sovereignty to slavery to service of the higher mandate of the collective soul quest for a covenant of prosperity into which human beings can live.

The nature of the soul is to evolve our bodies. The soul incarnates into the worlds of existence the potentials of the human spirit. It mediates the natural laws and the supernatural laws for the forming of human consciousness. This is a story of the forming of human consciousness through the fulfillment of soul potential and the creative intention that lives within reach of the human heart and mind.

The Spirit of America is born in this service.

Service

Service is an impulse within every human being that enables us to recognize our collective duty toward each other and to the world. It is a collective calling. It is the way spirit calls each of us to be intentionally attentive to the world. Service calls for a spontaneous creative act from within, in order to sustain or transform a given outer circumstance. It is essentially the art of being human, drawing on faculties within our soul-life, acknowledging our deepest relatedness as bearers and keepers for each other.

Service is the deepest form of friendship, a devotion to the archetypal impulse of humanity that becomes accessible through the act of two human beings co-creating together. Service is the highest initiation of our age: to live and work for the sake of the world.

Service is reciprocal. By living for each other, we create ourselves—if the world is one and humanity is one. It is our task to reveal this unity. Our task is to recreate this unity in every gesture, in every encounter. We are called to raise the world and each other.

Service is about providing the environment for the miraculous and living into it. We don't know how we will do the impossible. But we do a part, and somehow the rest happens. The co-creative hand of the spirit works in unison with our own efforts.

The service we do continues during sleep, when the beings that work on preserving and transforming life take hold of our efforts, our impulses, and weave them into world destiny. If we are awake to the nature of service, we will see that we are in relationship with spiritual beings outside our immediate environment.

Spiritual beings are service. The divine itself is service. When service is completed, grace and peace enter the world.

Importance of a loving heart on the path

A loving heart advances human development. It is a gift to the world. A loving heart is a recognition that allows us as human beings to remember larger dimensions of the same reality. It allows the past, present, and future to be understood within the time frame of now. It is a place from which I can act and decide for the greatest good for the greatest number of people and for the place where I stand. It brings one in service of something beyond one's own limitation. It provides and embodies a strength recognized as the aid of spiritual forces from the natural world and the supernatural world.

These forces aid us in fulfilling the everyday human task.

❋

The number of people that were removed from Africa for the purpose of slavery constituted depletion from the continent of the creative life forces that were necessary for the continuity of their social cultural practices. It was an undermining of the integrity of the cultural framework of these African communities of memory. The knowledge that supported the African way of life in Africa was primarily to keep a connection between the people and the ancestral world. Reality itself was constituted between the practical life and the ancestral memory, a memory accessed through the shrines and through ritual. This indigenous knowledge was integrated into the emerging cultural life in the Americas. Those Africans who were enslaved integrated the knowledge of their shrines into this new cultural reality in whatever way they could. This knowledge was not entirely lost but became hidden. The Africans' purpose behind hiding their spiritual knowledge was to ensure continuity of their practice. The way of hiding it created new forms of practice. It was hidden and accessed through symbolic systems of the Western spiritual tradition, including that of Christianity.

Once emancipation occurred, the African Gnostic stream continued to remain active, mostly outside of the political sphere. By remaining outside the political process, the security of the hidden inner processes that were supporting historical movements in America such as the Abolitionist movement, the Harlem Renaissance and the Civil Rights Movement was maintained. Different individuals and groups inspired each of those movements. These created agreements among themselves for the expression of new ways to transform this occult knowledge that was being practiced within these ritual initiation structures.

Initiation is an essential part of human development and social life. It maintains continuity of the spiritual forces that are shaping human development. In the absence of formal initiation, individuals and groups of people create experiences for themselves in an attempt to acknowledge this innate calling to be in touch with the spiritual world. Initiation is at the heart of the African worldview. It is a way of becoming oneself—connecting with the spiritual world of the ancestors and nature—a way to call forth an individual's purpose in life. Initiation means being fully formed. Once the Africans arrived in the New World, some systems were created that allowed individuals to experience an initiation path. These served as the processes for Africans' education and development. For Africans in America, finding freedom constituted an initiation path. For those who ran away from slavery and those who fought it on every level, this is considered an initiation path. Those who used the Abolitionist Movement and later the court systems in the restructuring of the political and social frameworks were influenced by the spiritual knowledge that constitutes the return of the soul to sovereignty.

The nature of the environment in which Africans were forced to live when they arrived in the Americas created a shift in how their shrines could be used to access the sacred places in the natural world and the ancestral world. The sacred is created by the intention the individual gives to accessing the natural elemental forces and utilizing them as a carrier of messages to the spiritual world. Even within the plantations and the cotton fields the act of invocation, through sound, particularly the spirituals that were sung, organized the elemental forces within the fields to act as an aid in the rituals of the African spiritual process. Fields were never empty of ritual because the use of words and sound and knowledge of the natural world was used for a great period of time during the enslavement of these Africans.

These various movements show the Africans journey from slavery to freedom and can be understood through the cultivation of a new initiatory experience. We are guided by the ancestral wisdom of what we must draw from the Earth to be free. The opening of the Earth shrines on the West Coast of Africa in 2000 to reconnect the lost soul forces of those who were removed from Africa and died in exile from their homeland served as a fulfillment of the ancestral prophecy that the Middle Passage inaugurated. It served as an entry point for a new age of humanity, a reconnection to the living potential of those who descended from these Africans.

This book holds a thread of my own initiation as it unfolded through stages of development and relationships. These served as a vessel for the ancestral spirits and memory to reveal themselves. It reveals my way of knowing how to overcome the boundaries of my own soul and social structures, to be able to attend to the call of spirit within our time. The book describes a way of learning beyond the cultural frameworks in which I live. The immersion into the natural and spiritual resources serves as the total environment for the human initiatory experience. It follows the tradition of *indaba*; a way of revealing what is shared through the processes of ritual and initiation. The spiritual practices invoke the deep knowledge of the soul and the beings within nature and the cosmos. The book's aim is to reveal through prophetic insights the task before not only the descendants of Africans in the Diaspora but also global humanity at a time of an emerging world potential.

This book is about service to the human social spiritual striving that unfolded through my encounter with youth who face the challenge of exclusion from the Promised Land. It holds a dedication of creating the beloved community embodied in the work of Dr. Martin Luther King Jr. through his methods of non-violence in the aim of strengthening the human will to serve a shared future. It serves to reconnect the larger aim of his vision and sacrifice to remove the veil, to live beyond the boundaries of fear and call forth the creative powers of human life.

This book tells a story of mentorship, my own and what I have provided as a context for helping others to return to the promise of spirit. The spirit inspires new agreements and the transformation of life. What it reveals is the hidden human path. The path that can arise out of the relational context that inspires us to participate in the modern initiation—hosting a reality we can share. It speaks to the effort to find the means to communicate into the various cultural frameworks, which allowed me to share an understanding of individuals from different cultural streams. It tells of the importance of places such as Brooklyn, New York; Watts, Los Angeles, and other cities where human communities struggle to coexist. This is the intention of the Shade Tree Multicultural Foundation, a community born out of the love of serving the potential of young people. And it describes the possibility for new currencies that aid the creative social life, wherein a rediscovery of initiation is made for the human collective. This occurs at the Seventh Shrine, *Imani*, the place of faith.

PART I
HISTORY AS INITIATION

I am Black as the night from which
the light of a new day descends.
I am past, present and future.
I am the anointed of heaven.
I am what I am.

I am the blended colors of life
that light the bridge into the new age.
I am seed, plant, and flower.
I am the anointed of Earth.
I am that I am.

—Anonymous

I

THE DARKNESS OF NIGHT

The quotation is the Serapis meditation given as an initiation text by Dr. Alfred Ligon, a Gnostic priest and founder of the Aquarian Spiritual Center. The meditation was conceived by him as a bridge between two cosmological ages—the Age of Pisces and the Age of Aquarius—and represents the people who served as the bridge. The two pillars on either side of the bridge represent the two ages and the symbolic processes in which human beings are initiated. Initiation takes place between what we know through tradition, which is the pathway of established spiritual truth, and the path of Gnosis connected to the underworld and to the dark night into which the human being must dream.

The pillar of tradition is the light of awareness in which the ancestral knowledge is transferred from one generation to the next. When tradition is lost, the human seed or spiritual essence enters into the realm of darkness. It creates a beginning for a new expression. This is the second pillar. It is a new impulse that enters the human spiritual stream rising out of the dark nature, the cosmic womb. The bridge is humanity that carries the seed of a new potential that serves to fulfill tradition. It creates the frameworks for the new possibilities of creation of the second pillar. When tradition is understood to its higher truths and when people are initiated into its wisdom, they become seers of the impulses within the darkness. They become prophets of the future age. Tradition cultivates for humanity the capacity for knowing the probabilities of what's hidden in the substance of the dark night.

Dr. Ligon referred to his synthesis of these traditions as Black Gnosticism, the initiation tradition originating in the African–Egyptian Mysteries. The word Gnosis from the Greek can be translated to mean the capacity for knowing. In the Gnostic traditions knowledge comes through intuition and a practice of meditation.

Serapis is the Egyptian God of the Underworld who guides the initiate through the passage of death into a new life. He opens the eyes and mouth of those that are blind and unable to speak. He restores their purpose by awakening the faculties for conscious knowing of the labyrinth of the underworld. He cultivates the awareness of the true powers of the soul and that process constitutes the resurrection of their free forces to ascend to the higher world. He guides them through the corridors of time to the portals of initiation of rebirth. When the soul forces are remembered rebirth occurs.

The Serapis meditation traces the symbolic language of the Egyptian myth and legends of creation and transformation. It is a retelling of the self-creative process through which the soul travels during manifestation and de-manifestation. It draws from the ancient traditions of the Mysteries where the powers of the soul utilize its self-creative process. The myth reveals the nature of the soul as the holder of knowledge through cultivated experiences and the free forces of the unmanifested powers of creation. When the soul is incarnated on the Earth a new initiation begins. The human being must remember to exercise the innate freedoms that the soul carries to fulfill the knowing that is embodied in the nature of its soul. This dialectic of remembering through a free initiative is the two pillars of initiation. The meditation was revealed to Dr. Ligon from his contemplation of the Osiris/Isis Mysteries, the passage of the soul through the underworlds and into the bodies of creation.

The legend of Osiris tells of the struggle between Osiris and his brother, Set, over Osiris's inheritance. Osiris ruled the upper world of the living and governed the throne of the Mysteries. He was the husband to Isis, the mother of the Universe and the keeper of the star wisdom. Set conspired to gain control over Osiris's realm and he invited Osiris to a banquet with the intention to kill him. Through his knowledge of the laws, Set dismembered his brother's body into fourteen pieces in order to keep his spirit from incarnating. The fourteen powers of creation that Osiris possessed were scattered throughout the sacred land of Egypt along the Nile so that Osiris would not be able to be enshrined or mummified for the preparation of resurrection. While Osiris was in the world of the dead suspended between death and resurrection, Set controlled his inheritance and governed his realm. Isis, through her immense devotion and love for Osiris, drew the pieces of his body together. She consulted with Thoth, the keeper of the Mysteries of life, who advised her on the ritual of restoring life to Osiris bringing his soul back into his body. Isis took her barge down the Nile and was able to find thirteen of the fourteen pieces. The missing part was the phallic powers that constituted the masculine force of creation. With a longing for a new way to bring life to Osiris she embraced his dead body with hers and awakened him with the creative powers of her heart. Osiris was revived into the world of the living for the purpose of seeing his creator, Isis. He then descended to the world of the dead as the priest of the new Mysteries, opening up the underworld to a new path of initiation that would allow those who would die after him to be guided to the path of rebirth.

INVOCATION

> *Infinite stars, infinite space, source of the knowledge of the worlds, giver of thoughts that empower creation, transforming light into the elements of matter, radiate before my mind the seven keys that unlock the doors of the Mystery Temple that I may enter and fulfill the purpose for which my birth initiates.*

The stars are the gold keys to the Mystery. They are the creative powers of thought, the awakening impulse that is aimed to the human soul. In some Gnosis traditions, stars are understood as beings that initiate humanity. They guide the incarnation of the powers of creation into the world of manifestation. The study of the stars is a symbolic language of the gods that reveals to man the past, present, and future forms of memory. In that sense they are the keepers of the record of the ages. They are the great Akashic field or the cosmic memory that supports the mental, psychic, and moral memory of the human being's initiation into life. The stars allow us to make contact with the beings that live amongst their brightness.

Meditation and contemplation are methods through which the human being makes contact with entities of the divine world—through which the qualities of these entities are released into the personality, into the soul and into the body. It constitutes initiation at its highest level. We are able to enter the gates of time through these constellations. We enter the worlds of the time spirits, the stars, in these fields of time—past, present, future—and constitute our memory by the light of intelligence. The stars guide the destiny of humanity not as a given fixed reality but through the cardinal law of creation. Through meditation and contemplation we can enter into a dialogue with the beings of light, life, and love. This intelligence of making contact with the stars and the world of spirit is the source of the known universe within the memory of humanity. They are our dream-keepers. They are the guides during the dark nights of our soul. They are the way-showers on the path of initiation. They are the gateways to the realms of immortality.

Within African traditions, ritual systems were established to align the human social life with the substances and powers of the natural and supernatural worlds. Nature served as a school for the cultivation of the cultural arts and sciences referred to as magic that allowed the African initiation systems to be developed. The arts and sciences of causing change to occur through the intention of ritual were consistent with the African way of life. These cosmologies hold within them visions of future events. The Earth is understood to be a field of dreams. The Earth receives from the ancestral and cosmological world the imagination. Imagination inspires human beings to co-create the realities into which we live. The Earth coalesces for human beings life and the light that emanates from the star beings, giving us the understanding of what we must do to move the realms of possibility into the now. As human beings, we act as dreamcatchers when we extend our minds toward the Mysteries.

Dreaming is living beyond one's time into future and allowing the body to absorb the substances inherent in the powers of light. To imagine is to awaken to the possibilities that stretch far beyond the given frameworks of what exists. It is to invoke in thought and in will the powers of creation for what is to come. Prophecy is the embodiment of the intention to serve something that will be in the world in a future time because we can decipher it now. Gnosis is the process of enlivening the mind with what is to come. Gnosis, the act of knowing through meditation and contemplation, enables preparation for the necessary acceptances for what is possible. Through the process of initiation we are able to experience subtle and higher levels of creation. The prophetic mind is synonymous with Gnosis and sees into the acts of creation as it unfolds before us. This occurs when we align our highest intentions with the natural laws that govern the worlds of existence, which we experience through our own bodies.

Divination is an art of reading the cosmograms. The natural rhythms of daily life within the world are perfected through the intentional investigation of the natural laws, giving us the ability to interpret the probability of future events. It is a conversation of putting before the spiritual world our thoughts and asking them to reveal what we don't know.

The mind is understood to be the space between the stars. It is the darkness that constitutes the womb that gives birth to the star beings. Meditation is a way of accessing the womb of creation. Meditation allows the human being to recall the primary act of beginning. Meditation allows us the epigenesis of thought and the law of divination. *Theurgy* is the spiritual science of the ancient Egyptians. The mind is a field that we can navigate with intention. We can make contact with the beings of the higher worlds and the realms of nature. Thus we formulate our systems of knowledge. The mind is a holy substance that fills the space between the stars, sustaining and revitalizing their existence. For the ancient Egyptians it gave rise to the symbolic text and verses known as hieroglyphics, the language of *Ptah*. The creative utterance gives rise to forms and the world of manifestation. *Ptah* is the word giver and the power of prophecy, what will be.

The Word

Creation and Manifestation require laws. Principles determine how things are formed and how they are manifested. This process of giving form and purpose to a reality is called the Word. All sacred acts that have been recorded for human traditions embody the power of the Word. The Word is the source for what is created. The Word is what is sustained in the realms of creation. The Word is the force that transforms creation after creation has fulfilled its purpose. The Word is a giving gesture because the Word facilitates the giving of meaning. The Word expresses the power of creation and it constitutes life, the giver of reality. The Word releases life into the world of existence. Life that remains above and beyond the dimension of nature comes into nature, both the nature of the human being and the nature of the world through the Word. The Word releases the divinity into the world of perception. When meaning fills into this space of consciousness, the human being adds creation to nature. The Word is a creative power behind human life. The Word becomes revealed and then becomes real, becomes manifest. So when we speak we give to the world something it has never had, and cannot have without human speech. Speech and the Word are the various gestures we make, not just language, as the Word can be any artistic expression.

Human speech invokes the self. Human speech awakens the self to be present. The nature of speech is not just to communicate words or ideas, but to communicate presence. The nature of speech communicates the reality that can be borne out of what I say. My saying is an activity that becomes a doing once it becomes understood and felt. When I am listening to something that is being said I create mental pictures out of what I hear. I bring into myself insight derived from the meaning of the spoken words.

My speech embodies me as a human entity. I become what I say. So speech begins on the energetic level of the human being and includes all the various dimensions of human life processes. This begins with the physical organs that allow for the capacity for speech. It extends into the psychic realm to be able to include another human being. The Word sets up the context. It includes the possibility of time, because I may be speaking in the past, present, or future tense. And these are specific levels of the imagination and memory that allow us to constantly create and recreate the domain of reality. In a sense speech is not just the literal language constructs, but the meaning that we give to everything we do is speech. Every movement that a human engages in is speech. We're the host and the guest of this power of speech.

Indaba

"I have something important to tell you." *Indaba* is a Zulu word that was introduced to me by Credo Mutwa, a Zulu

Sanusi. *Indaba* involves the technique of using the Word to awaken the deep memory within the bodies and minds of people. When I was with Credo Mutwa in South Africa, I was initiated into the tradition of *indaba*, a way of invoking and making contact with human beings and beings in other realms. Credo Mutwa asked me to use *indaba* in creating a space in the work I do with young people through Shade Tree Multicultural Foundation. So in our work mentoring young people through Shade Tree we don't call it a meeting or group process, we call it *indaba*, which means deep talk.

Indaba is connected to the Star Mystery tradition in Africa. It includes divination and is also storytelling. Elders utilize *Indaba* when they gather to determine the business for the community life. It occurs when the elders gather the youth together to teach the traditional knowledge. *Indaba* is a counsel and an investigation into something that requires deep understanding or insight. It is also a trial—justice is passed through *indaba*. But in an *indaba*, it's expected that justice will be present. And justice is not just an application of man-made laws, but *indaba* is a way of looking at the archetypal laws that govern human life. *Indaba* is a structure that can be utilized for the clarification and purpose of a person's life circumstance. It is more like a ritual healing and we create sanctuary for that through *indaba*. We create a space for other levels of truth to be present.

So the word *indaba* carries the power of the Word. What happens is that the imagination around *indaba* presupposes that the outcome will be deeper than the everyday conversation. What is being shared is something that has to do with the total life of the person. In the process of mentoring we expect and hold that space intentionally for that process. So when we use the word *indaba* we know that we're going toward a particular depth of sharing. We take responsibility to make that happen.

Mentoring is conversation of the heart, dialogue from the heart: "Deep talk." The nature of *indaba* is for the person to be able to enter their own story, their own biography, as well as their own history—not the history that just goes back into their personal history, but the history that goes down, into the deeper life memory, into the soul memory.

I like it also to mean, "I give you my word." There is an understanding of honesty and a certain type of imagination, to dream into this future, and to decide for the best—to decide for a probability that would fulfill one's life needs, life circumstances.

Indaba is an awakening. It's a question about what if? As a focal point for mentorship it is about creating a conversation for the possibilities to be shared and the dream to be entertained in the visioning process of the lives of individuals and groups.

SAWUBONA

My sense of place and time in the world comes about by meeting people—in meeting something in each person that becomes awakened through eye contact and through the gesture of proximity. It is best described by a word the Zulu people use in Southern Africa. The word is *sawubona*—a word we can translate into English by saying, "We see you." We acknowledge that I'm not just an individual. I'm part of an ancestral vision. I'm part of a future possibility of seeing how I can be in the world. Today *sawubona* is probably just a common everyday greeting in most places, but historically it was a word that intended to awaken people. When one person greets another and says *sawubona* (we see you), the response is *Yebo sawubona* (Yes, we see you, too). In this mutual seeing the two individuals take up something that can only be possible by the acknowledgement of the word *sawubona*. That I'm not just seeing you physically but I'm asking you, "Do you remember me?" or "Do you remember the time that we had set to meet?" "And are you willing to take up what can be critically engaged between us?" So the word holds several significant meanings simultaneously. It puts human beings in touch with something, not just speech. It puts human beings in touch with the relatedness to speech as the creative act of will. This becomes an agreement for a mutual way of looking toward the future, toward what we can collectively give and share.

This book is an *indaba* on the enslavement of the African people, their forced initiation in the Middle Passage through their journey from their homeland on the continent of Africa across the waters of the Atlantic to the shores of a new place. Dr. Martin Luther King in his speech "I Have a Dream," revealed the gift carried by these Africans in their souls' longing for a renewed sense of belonging. The belonging that we are looking for is a sense of our agreement about our place within society, nature, and the cosmos. This is the Promised Land available to every human being and every place where human beings cohabit. It refers to our sense of a shared reality where we find the common ground for our daily experience of living.

This journey is also a personal journey into the deep memory of my own soul and into the stories of those whose lives guide me and enable me to serve the Dream.

I step through the door of no return to wade into the water, to be a cargo in the bowels of night traveling through time and the undercurrents of grief pulled by a longing for return. I awake only to the stars that guide my faithful heart to the ancestral world. Their patient voices sing to me, to rest, to remember. I wait for day beyond my lifetime, beyond my children's lifetime in which I will emerge to plant in this new earth the seeds that I have carried in my firm grip as a sower of the ancestral promise.

2

THE MIDDLE PASSAGE

History and Traditions

The Middle Passage, the journey of peoples from the African continent to the Americas, took place from approximately the mid–1500s to the mid–1800s. It was called the Middle Passage because European ships brought trade items from Europe to Africa in exchange for slaves. The slaves were carried on the middle leg of the journey to the Americas. The slaves were exchanged for goods to be brought back to Europe. The Middle Passage and the dispersion of Africans into the larger world space through forced migration is estimated to have included close to a hundred million people. Approximately twenty-eight million made it alive. But for every one that survived, three died on the way. They died in the interior of Africa fighting to prevent capture. They died on the journey from the interior to the coasts of Africa. They died from the wait in the dungeons or during the passage itself. It was a brutal process. We can say that Africans were forced not just to migrate but to transmigrate. Africans were forced to set into motion a dream that became a collective power in the psychic life of millions of people who had to relocate heritage and history and seed culture in a future that they didn't know would come to be.

The indigenous mind maintains an active co-creative presence with every given circumstance in which the human individual finds him or herself. For traditional African people the world of reality is never finished; rather, reality is a place where messages show up through symbolic and sacred acts that engage the will of African people. The Middle Passage, over time, allowed those Africans who maintained the ancestral memory and the active process of indigenous wisdom to formulate strategies for perpetuating their existence in a future that would not follow the predictable patterns of their enslavement. Their ritual imagination enabled them to intuit such a future. It drew from nature and cosmos the substances that allowed these Africans to transcend the hardships of slavery and to participate in the epigenesis of a new world reality.

Slavery changed the outer forms of the enslaved Africans' social existence. Slavery deferred their dream of freedom to a future time. Their immediate task was to transform the rituals and symbolic systems they had brought with them from Africa into new forms.

These new forms would allow them to recover their humanity in their present circumstances. This included the integration of their spiritual systems with Christianity. The plantation served as both a place for their enforced labor and, paradoxically, as the place where they wove their destiny. The rituals performed by the slaves with the earth of the plantation were consistent with the rituals they had experienced in their homeland. The elemental world was still accessible. The ritual practice of invoking it through song was still available. The

Christian spirituals they sang hid words and tones that shaped the course of events within the natural world and within the limited social structures that the slaves controlled. Freedom was inevitable to them. Freedom was inevitable because of their access to these natural resources and the spiritual rituals that were reestablished within the new cultural cosmology. Their knowledge of earth shrines was woven into their daily work in the soil of the plantations. In spite of their bondage, the slaves still had the freedom to create. Every initiation brings forth gifts from the spiritual world into the human soul and mind as an awareness of what to decide for in the worlds of manifestation. The forced initiation of African peoples in the New World brought forth the gift of second sight. It was this capacity to see beyond their own time, which fostered an agreement within the consciousness of the enslaved African that the dream of freedom would be realized in the future.

Traditional Cultures

When we speak of African traditional culture, we do not mean merely a preservation of the past or the status quo, as the word tradition now typically implies. In fact, this usual interpretation of the word tradition helps maintain the appearance of reality—not actual reality—so some people may appear to be religious or creative when they're not. To some degree, merely preserving inherited frameworks annihilates the capacity for improvisation. When we refer to indigenous cultures as "traditional societies," we should know that they were traditional, not simply in maintaining the status quo. Their essential nature was founded on constantly attuning with the natural cycles of time and place. Their rituals incorporated those rhythms into their daily life. The true cultural processes inherent in indigenous traditions embody the capacity to formulate rituals that access the natural, cosmological, and spiritual worlds, including all the changes that inevitably entails.

Initiation

At the core of African traditions lies initiation—the process of remaking the covenants between the ancestral spiritual world and the human social world, thereby renewing the frameworks that support daily life. Initiation integrates individuals into the community. Initiation serves as a larger context for bringing forth the spiritual, creative resources endowed in the collective cosmology. Initiation provides the continuity between the changes from one phase to another in the unfolding of the cultural process. During the process of initiation, the human individual is immersed in the ancestral spiritual world—so that self-knowledge and purpose can be awakened. Inherent in every human being is his or her social task or purpose within the community. In the absence of initiation, however, this remains latent and forgotten. To live without initiation creates a distortion in one's sense of self and one's sense of place. Living without initiation leads to self-destructive acts and violence toward the other.

Every human community had a way of initiating its members into the agreements that promote the common good. Initiation awakens people to the understanding of what they carry within themselves that supports this common good. African peoples in the Americas were forced to abandon many essential attributes of tradition, which included language, rituals, and their shrines. Without the spiritual ritual practices that kept active the memory of the larger potential between the social and spiritual realms, significant resources for a higher quality of life were forgotten and lost. Those who were initiated, however, sustained and kept secret, as best they could, the knowledge of their ancestors and of nature. They utilized this knowledge by merging it with the approved spiritual and social norms of the predominant culture.

This capacity for initiation unfolds within the soul the continuity of the human spiritual element. It is beyond the body and material forms of existence. Initiation takes place in the spiritual world. Initiation finds its place within the soul and further manifests as culture. The group of Africans that crossed the Atlantic found themselves within a dimension of time and place unknown and uncertain. This absence of homeland meant that they had to create a new way of life—one that would enable them to meet their new spiritual task. Those with the capacity of seer-ship who were present onboard the vessels coming to the Americas engaged in ritual initiation of their fellow captives. They taught them to see deeply into the world into which they were traveling. They taught them to learn to traverse the depths of the ocean they were crossing. They taught them to divine through the stars how to find a way home.

The Africans' presence in this new world caused a reformulation of new rituals of becoming. A structuring of new shrines embodied their memory and collective purpose. They were never without the ancestral presence. The ancestral presence forged a new form of initiation within the soul. This new way of being was revealed in *The Souls of Black Folk* by W. E. B. Du Bois as the birth of a seventh son—those gifted with second sight who could see within and without the veil of material reality. They were able to read into destiny many possibilities of the future generations, who would carry this soul capacity to make use of higher spiritual laws grounded in practical ritual magic—their natural spiritual science of becoming themselves.

> *After the Egyptian and Indian, the Greek and Roman, the Teuton and Mongolian, the Negro is a sort of seventh son, born with a veil, and gifted with second sight in this American world—a world which yields him no true self-consciousness, but only lets him see himself through the revelation of the other world.* (W. E. B. Du Bois, *The Souls of Black Folk,* p. 9)

The teaching of the esoteric or occult view of African peoples within the American frame of life begins with the African understanding of it. Their cosmology informs how they see and experience reality. The Middle Passage became more than an act of enslavement. Africans resisted the enslavement on many levels. Those who found themselves captured into its structure found it necessary to use their own occult knowledge. This knowledge directed other probabilities of how they could survive and prepare capacities for the future of their descendants. On their journeys to North America and the Caribbean, elders would get onboard the ships and initiate people into the milieu, the journey itself. They initiated them in a transformational water ritual. In so doing, the elders merged the people with the larger spiritual potential of what this initiation became.

The actual passage became an initiatory rite for many of the people who had been chosen on the ship to enter the water ritual of moving through the currents of time. The ocean itself became a vessel through which a passage occurred for the soul to transform. It is not surprising that these aspects of the history are today so little known. In my exploration of this theme, I found that there are not many elders in Africa who would share details of what those rituals were. Up until 1998, the rituals were still actually taking hold, taking form. So for 400 years, the initiation of this soul process was an active process still occurring. It was only at the end of 1998, at a time of a prophetic mandate, that the elders of the Earth shrines on the Western Coast of Africa participated in rituals initiating the closure of the Middle Passage and initiating a new covenant.

The Middle Passage created one of the larger outpourings of grief within the frameworks of human history. The extractions of tens of millions of people from their place of origin and the context of their meaningful existence constituted a great loss. The death of millions poured into the ancestral world a mighty call for help. This event of the Middle Passage was seen in the spiritual world as a call to the ancestors to come directly into the experience of this loss. Grief is an opening to the other world. It is a call to the forces of nature and cosmos to aid human beings when we are most vulnerable. Grief is a submersion in the latent powers of the soul, in order to awake to higher levels of striving to substantiate our true purpose. It leads to the initiation threshold and serves as an intelligence to bring us—individually and collectively—to decisions about our future. Grief awakens us to our purpose and our path.

Through the heightened state of consciousness brought on by grief, we find within our daily life an awareness of something new spontaneously arising out of our contact with the Earth. The Earth is a creative intelligence that supports human existence through what it provides for physical life as well as our spiritual destiny. The ecology of the Earth, its natural laws, supports the ecology of consciousness, what we perceive and cognize as reality. It provides for us the foundation of our capacity to know. The Earth liberates for us the inner powers of human life. The natural laws inherent in the Earth are inherent in the body. The Earth restores and revitalizes the human capacity of will power through the force we call magnetism, the capacity to attract the powers of creation and light into the body. The human entity through consciousness organizes the creative forces into world existence. The Earth is the foundation for the human will to reenter the covenants that are the frameworks for life itself. The tremendous pain and the loss of human life experienced by African peoples in slavery evoked through grief a deep spiritual connection to the place in which they found themselves. Grief evokes from the Earth a creative force that can be called a shrine.

Geomancy and Earth Shrines

These Earth shrines are covenants between a people, the place where they are on the Earth, and their relationship to the ancestral world. The African knowledge of the Earth consists of knowing it as an elemental field, a field through which we communicate with the ancestors, with the spirits of nature, and the elemental forces of creation. The enslavement of these African people engaged them directly in an earthly task of cultivating plantations for the commerce of the newly established slave states. Consistent with their tradition, Africans wove into this work their rituals. They sang into the earth their ancestral songs and thereby cultivated, not just the land, but their future as well. Their work in the fields became a way to establish their Earth shrines, so the plantations became places of dreams and the seeds of the prophecy of the Promised Land were sown there.

The Earth carries within it a capacity to make human beings indigenous wherever they are, not just in their native land or place of birth. To be indigenous in this deeper sense is to reformulate one's body in order to draw from the Earth the creative will power to be oneself and to fulfill one's purpose and destiny in a particular place. The Earth can become a portal of initiation that gives us an exact coordinate for our path of life. It restores the sense of home. It provides our departure point for what we call our soul's striving. The Earth orients us to the ultimate purpose and nature of existence, to be here now, and to fulfill our higher calling. The Earth gives us the creative powers of the place where we find ourselves. We're always at home when we know the nature of the Earth and how to access the powers it offers us.

The prophecy of the Promised Land speaks to the capacities of a person or a group of people to give to a place their gifts. It is a covenant between human groups and the powers of a place. The Promised Land is understood to be what becomes probable in human existence when we decide for our freedom. Ultimately this is a freedom to give meaning to our existence in alignment with the purpose of the place we inhabit, a Homeland. Within our collective striving we participate in a social, spiritual endeavor. The endeavor creates a sense of home, of belonging, and a sense of giving to the Earth our will. The Earth is then a witness and a host of human creative acts. The place where we live becomes an Earth shrine.

Geomancy is the study of the Earth forces and processes that allow human beings to know the changes that the Earth generates. It is a spiritual science of reading the time currents flowing through the Earth, which can be found in most traditional cultural and ritual systems. It enables practitioners to access knowledge about the elemental beings living within the frameworks of the natural ecology of the Earth. And it can be used to effect changes in relationship to our will through practical science and ritual magic. The science of Geomancy helps us to locate the minerals, the element of water, and the element of fire that the Earth carries. It is a prophetic science of seeing into the subtle realms.

Every geographic space supports unique qualities that we may call culture. Human beings organize their daily life based on what they draw from that geographic reality. The North American continent can be understood as a being or a collective of spiritual beings with distinct qualities, who affect human perception and cognition. The forces that flow through this continent awaken the human will to strive, especially, for a quality of freedom. It was already within the traditions of the indigenous peoples of this land to agree with the principles of peace, which are present as an inherent force within the natural ecology of North America.

The indigenous wisdom of North America tells of the beings from the four directions that lead humanity to a deeper understanding of the sacred medicine that is called peace.

The nature of living within the framework of this indigenous ground we call North America is to serve the beings of peace, to be initiated into their mysteries, to be transformed into a consciousness of giving. The people of various human cultures that have found their way to this continent—those coming from Europe, Asia, and Africa—have gone through a process of becoming aware of the various potentials within the reality of this land. Each group has had to work out for themselves what it means to live into the deeper substance of what this land provides. Freedom on every level is an essential self-evident truth, which is a goal of initiation. Slavery of African peoples could not be sustained as a cultural, political and economic reality in America. The nature and the prophetic power of the place would not allow it.

People became free, not only because of political developments, but also through the nature of the land. Even though the sociopolitical frameworks were not given to support liberty for the slaves, their inner soul forces became endowed with the forces of freedom. It was their inner striving that allowed them to know about the Promised Land and inwardly to prepare for it. It was not a politically created state, but one that arises out of free soul forces. The Promised Land—for all of us, as for them—is determined by the choice we make to be ourselves, beyond the conditions of exploitation.

Once the initiates who survived the Middle Passage reached the Americas, they established Earth shrines here. These shrines were where memory is virtually stored in trees and areas close to rivers, where rituals continued to be developed, and where initiations took place, including the submersion of people under water. Such shrines still exist in the places these first African-Americans lived. There are some off the coast of Georgia; the Gullah communities still have traditions tied to them. Shrines still exist as well in the Caribbean: in Cuba, Haiti, Jamaica, and Brazil.

The places where these Earth shrines have been established will become more obvious as the Earth changes continue. They will, in time, become recognized as places that provide us access to the deeper memory of the ancestral world and the prophecies hidden within them. We are now witnessing, in this time of radical transition, a transfer of this ancestral substance into the world, initiating soul capacities that will aid us in connecting directly to the world of spirit and the world of nature. The element of water was thought to be the bringer of this new energy for the awakening of those who carry the legacy of this cultural sacrifice of slavery. The ancestral waters, as they are called, come as rain to the places that are inspirited with this elemental force. Water is the psychic presence of the activity of the future making its way into the world. The cultural significance of this will be revealed in the unfolding of new capabilities to co-create with nature, the worlds of the ancestors, and the worlds of cosmic beings. New realities will unfold that will honor the true nature and dignity of the human spirit. We are at the beginning of the covenant of a new era of human life.

3

MAKING THE NEW COVENANTS

There was and still is no justification for human slavery, genocide of tens of millions of people, and the systematic destruction of their traditions and cultural life. The African holocaust did occur and its impact is still felt on the African continent and among the peoples of the Diaspora. The intent here is to make a distinction in relationship to initiation and purpose of life. Initiation itself is separation from a state of continuity, of everything familiar and secure into a state of disruption, uncertainty, and dilemma. Life itself necessitates initiation. It is not that African people could not find other pathways for initiation. Yet the experience of slavery became by necessity a process of initiation.

The Africans brought with them their understanding of the purpose of life—to utilize all ancestral knowledge, knowledge of nature and of the cosmos in order to sustain their collective and individual destiny. The making of a new life is the African way when radical change happens. The first and second steps in an initiatory process known as the separation and dilemma phases occurred as a result of the forced migrations of Africans into the slavery experience. The length of time in which Africans experienced slavery in America was dramatically different from any previous disruption in their cultural story. The scale of this human drama both in measure of human loss and cultural disruption created one of the largest potential changes in recent human memory caused by human intent.

The third phase and the most significant in the completion in an initiatory experience is the return, the homecoming, the process of awakening to what the separation and dilemma phases have created. The nature of the soul and the purpose of life are to transform existence into capacities for freedom, including the freedom to sacrifice for something greater than one's individual sense of purpose, to serve the whole unfolding of the powers of creation.

African cosmologies were intended to sustain natural and spiritual realities contained within the life bodies and ancestral memories of the people. In the early phases of the slavery experience there was sufficient knowledge of the traditions to be able to transfer the fundamental principles of ritual and initiation into the new context of their lives. This hidden aspect of the African sojourn in America and the places of the Diaspora sustained their spiritual connection to the ancestral shrines and knowledge, and fortified their potential for another kind of freedom distinct and separate from the political as well as cultural freedoms that were denied to them. Within the slavery system, efforts were made to sustain this contact with their spiritual tradition by assimilating it into the dominant cultural forms and into the natural environment that supported their existence.

The assimilation of the African spiritual systems with Christianity included adapting the various deities in the pantheon of African cosmology to the saints in Christian theology and to the nature of Christianity itself. Ritual systems in daily life such as birth rituals, marriages, and funerals took on the subtle influences of African tradition. The new rituals were about sustaining life and the purpose of life in order to be in contact with the natural and spiritual realities above everything else. The nature of the mind is to be in contact with the dream, and the indigenous mind could not be separated from it. However, because of the limited social freedoms and the suppressed ritual experiences, the dream, individual and collective, had to be deferred during the long struggle for freedom, which in many ways is still ongoing.

The ancestral world became more present to the indigenous memory of Africans in the Americas and the indigenous peoples of these lands with the genocide that groups experienced. The dramatic loss of life, in the absence of the rite of passage for the dead into the realms of the ancestors, resulted in the dead living within the veil of the everyday world. The disembodied human spirits that did not reach the spiritual thresholds of their destiny remained within the realms of nature and within proximity of the living.

Life is intention, the cultivation of a memory to fulfill a creative and purposeful existence. This purpose can form itself beyond the limits of physical life to the degree that the soul's spiritual nature strives to complete the initiation for which it was born. It is known through the teachings of the elders who remained connected to the world of the dead that the American Epoch, which includes slavery and the genocide of the indigenous peoples of this land, created a sphere of life known as the World of the Dead. It is active and influential in what we create as future.

This sphere constitutes a prophecy that the ancestral world would inspire the awakening of their descendants to know the nature of the ancestral sacrifice. By knowing the nature of the sacrifice the cultivated soul has the capacity to create a reality based on the right use of soul powers gained through initiation. The right use of soul powers is to be able to live in the covenant of the ancestral dream. This new radical initiatory experience fostered a capacity for spiritual gifts to be cultivated by one person and be given to another.

What transpired in the initiatory experience of African people was the creation of the soul spiritual capacity that would be gifted to generations of the future through the cultivation of an Earth shrine that is their inheritance. The transference of that legacy is not from an individual soul from one lifetime to the next but as a collective soul experience from one person to the next. The ancestors were now living for their descendants the powers to choose what level of freedom they must strive for and attain. There was a new covenant between those who died within the experience of slavery and those who were alive within the Veil. The intention of subsequent initiation systems was to remove the Veil between the mental, psychical capacities of life to allow people to recall the soul knowledge inherited from their ancestral sacrifice.

How does the emancipated African become part of the American stream? The places where the Africans were enslaved now had the shrines. Connections had been reestablished with the traditional shrines and some ritual systems had been redeveloped. At the point of Emancipation the work needed was to develop social and cultural systems in order to utilize the ancestral memory and to participate in the possibilities of the emerging American experience. The two spiritual streams that were now forged during this time were the African Gnosis connected to the African indigenous memory and the new soul qualities emerging from the deeper American spiritual impulse, which was the indigenous understanding of peace. There were two spiritual strivings occurring within formal and informal initiation systems in America. The formal structures took on the establishment of political and cultural frameworks for a nation state that would support the primary freedoms of an individual supported by the rights of Constitutional Law. It had within it the Rosicrucian and Masonic traditions, which carried the European spiritual and traditional mandates. Among the majority of people seeking social freedoms—Africans, Native Americans, and white immigrants—the informal initiation arising from the suffering and difficulties of social life created the criteria for a distinct form of justice and social spiritual freedom, a love for a shared future.

The Constitutional framework was understood to carry more than statehood and human rights. It was understood that many of the founding members of the American democratic ideals recognized this spiritual significance of African experience in America and supported the creation of opportunities for the integration of this impulse. These included Benjamin Franklin, Abraham Lincoln, and the work of the esotericist and Rosicrucian Pascal Beverly Randolph, who framed for the American leadership the deeper understanding of the gift that blacks hold for America's future.

African presence in America ushered in the need for the acknowledgement of what the African presence added to the collective destiny of America. What is the social task before the African people and how do they integrate their spiritual legacy? The Africans were not without their initiatory guides and methods of accessing their traditional wisdom. They utilized techniques for preserving the rites of passage and finding ways to imbue their traditions with new symbolic systems, into thought and practice. They understood Emancipation beyond freedom from slavery—the realization of creating a new cosmology and perfecting the deeper wisdom of what was hidden in the earth of the American experience. They called forth a future from this in which nature and culture collaborated to provide them access to a new way of life. Among the collective were elders, holders of knowledge, who tried to hold the strategy of this collective group impulse so that they might find purpose and meaning after Emancipation from slavery.

The Abolitionist Movement had within it members of the Rosicrucian Society, an extension of the European Masonic stream, and those African Gnostic initiates who sought methods to utilize the higher laws and the spiritual legacies that were now being accessed for the creating of a nation. Their collective aim was to secure initiation forms that would allow those freed from slavery to be able to enter formal education to develop the soul capacities and to exercise a measure of creative activity within the social spheres and emerging religious systems within the culture. These included the forming of churches, universities, lodges, and other cultural institutions that would support the collective striving. The leading teachers took up the deeper meaning of the Constitution of the United States, pointing to the human potential to create freedoms out of soul capacities, during the Reconstruction Era. This was in addition to the work of the political activists that carried the social task. There were initiation systems in the cultural institutions that worked to integrate these spiritual qualities into the American stream.

The outspoken abolitionist Pascal Beverly Randolph was born in 1825 in Virginia to William Beverly Randolph and Flora Beverly, an African woman who may have been descended from Madagascan royalty. Randolph traveled extensively throughout Europe and into the Middle East studying spiritualism. He also trained as a physician. While on a trip to England in 1858 he was made the Rosicrucian Supreme Grand Master of the Western World and Knight of the Ordre du Lys. After returning to the United States he founded the first Rosicrucian organization in the United States.

In 1851, P. B. Randolph became acquainted with Abraham Lincoln through the Rosicrucian Fraternity, where organization records reveal that they evidently served together with General Ethan Allen on the Great Council. From Randolph, Lincoln learned that seeded in the African-American story, psyche, and soul life, lay a significant reality for the future of America. This future had been what the Africans cultivated in their soul life through the initiation of slavery. Freeing the slaves was in the best interests of strengthening the foundation of American ideals and to allow for the release of the Africans' creative potential into a free relationship with the economic, civil, and political life of America.

Randolph explored the world of the dead, the world of the ancestors, and formulated a mystery school to cultivate the soul capacity of those descended from this slavery experience. As the head of the Rosicrucian movement in the Western Hemisphere, he organized the initiatory platform to bring about the development of the souls of black folks. The

Emancipation of slavery supported the political destiny of the American South by transforming the institution of slavery. With Randolph's influence it also catalyzed Africans' contribution to the industrial revolution and the artistic life within America. Pascal Beverly Randolph influenced the role of the Freedmen's Bureau after the Emancipation of the slaves so that it became an institution to assign rights and privileges not just for forty acres and a mule but to also administer the rites of passage into the Masonic tradition. Randolph founded the first lodge for African Americans to initiate them into the political sphere. Due to Lincoln's death and the subsequent problems in Reconstruction, these goals were not fully realized; however, various impulses survived. Some of the early African American organizations that were formed, including the United Negro Improvement Association founded by Marcus Garvey, had those rights and privileges established as a result of the knowledge of this deeper covenant.

The established rights and privileges within these newly formed institutions were intended to support the third phase of the initiation process—the return to self-governance through the investment of social agreements that allow people to exercise control over their destiny. The social rights supported through the Constitution were understood as the basic given tenets for other freedoms that would become available to the people through practice and agreements made out of their free will. However, racism had been institutionalized and prevented the exercise of this free will for the creation of a more authentic American society.

The inherent agreement of peace that is the underlying impulse of this continent, its indigenous wisdom and the cultural sacrifice of many groups of people was now challenged by a system of cultural privilege controlled by one dominant group over others. This social power of the state and the established privilege of race and class limited the free expression of people of color and at the same time undermined the higher purpose of those who identified as white. Their cultural worldview of white supremacy and racism seeded into the psyche of whites in general an attitude of fear in the encounter with people of color.

The social task taken up by Americans in this particular time who specifically identified themselves as white, instead of through their ancestral memory and places of origin, was no longer focused on the ideals of freedom, initiation, and the deep agreements around human creative possibilities. Instead this task became an institutionalizing of white identity and the cultural political powers assigned to it to control human and natural resources, to limit human development, and to restrict healthier forms of economy and self-sufficiency. Race became the basis for civil conflict and social violence characteristic of American society. These forces can only be transformed by the indigenous and initiatory wisdom of the nature of the place where we find ourselves, this continent that carries a dream of peace, the collective agreements for higher human potential, and the spiritual creativity drawn from the ancestral sacrifice.

PART II

PERSONAL INITIATION

Destiny is the path we are called to follow. To awaken to destiny is to awaken to our vocation, to our true name, which is the unique possibility of our own being and what we have been given. Awakening to our calling, we grasp our predisposition to give and to return what we have been given. Destiny reminds us to be present, attentive, and responsive to the needs of the world. It is a gradual process, unfolding as we cultivate the capacities that are drawn out by the encounters, both inner and outer, that we are given.

Destiny is remembrance of the self. To remember the self is to meet the self, which is to uncover the predisposition to give. It is what we are, what life is about—realizing the gift we are and returning it. This is love. Conscious love awakens destiny, as consciousness of destiny awakens love. Destiny begins with the gift of "first" love—our mother's love, which gives us the primal intuition of relatedness, a recognizable truth that sustains the story of our humanity by transforming the boundaries and limitations of the given. When love becomes conscious, "first" love evolves into "second" love—the love that we give.

Our individual destiny cannot be fully realized if it is isolated from other people's biographies and other people's stories. We know ourselves as a result of knowing others who help shape and share our worldview, affecting our thinking, our feeling, and our will.

Imagining the story of our lives, we allow the significance of our being to emerge. Everyone is called to discover the unique meaning in his own life.

4
THE BEGINNING OF THE PERSONAL PATH

DESTINY

Guyana was one of the first countries in the Americas to be established as a slave trade colony. The Dutch settled it in 1616 followed by the English in 1791. Beginning in the mid–1700s in Guyana, there was resistance against slavery and colonialism. The abolition of slavery by Britain in 1792 led to the establishment in Guyana of certain cultural rights, which did not develop into full political rights until the 1900s. Guyana finally gained its independence from Britain in 1966. Despite the long period of colonialism, many of the traditions brought by enslaved Africans were and are very present in the folk culture through the stories, food, music, dance, and birth and death.

I was born in Linden, Guyana, in 1966, the sixth of seven children in a tightly knit nuclear family that operated within the orbit of a large extended family. Some of our relatives lived with us; others joined us on a daily or special-occasion basis.

Though there were economic difficulties, my childhood provided me with a great sense of stability and security. As siblings, we were close and spent a lot of time doing things together and with friends. My mother provided spiritual guidance for the family and a religious structure for the younger siblings. Education was an essential element of our family values as was music. We had a piano at home and frequently sang together.

Two months after I was born, the family moved to Georgetown, the capital and largest city in Guyana. Even in the city, nature was close at hand. Everyone had a yard full of fruit trees. We were close to the ocean, so our weekends were filled with walking to the beach for recreation or to one of the many botanical gardens around the city. Nature was very accessible to us as children. The natural world was where we played, where we sought discoveries, and where I experienced the presence of spirit.

One of the things I loved was that Guyanese culture is centered on the sharing that occurred during meals and community time. There was always extended family life, which I enjoyed as well—visiting cousins and spending time away from home with other relatives. I loved the deep friendships that I experienced and the storytelling that filled our days as children, as well as sports and play.

Many questions emerged in my life from what I experienced daily. The night was alive with wonder, even more so because our electric power was unreliable and we often lived by candlelight. The natural environment was more dynamic than the man-made cultural space. Night was really dark and the stars were unbelievably bright. I witnessed the incredible power of thunderstorms, the amazing display of the animal life, and the migration of tens of thousands of birds. I was aware of sounds of insect life both throughout each day and during the different seasons.

When I was a child I did not always feel part of the culture of Guyana. I was aware of things that were not taught or spoken about. As an adult I realize that there are aspects of reality that most people do not experience. I, as a child, however, had a different level of access. I woke up with a certain level of intensity to be connected to something that allowed my daily rhythm to be guided. My attention was strongest in the morning because I wanted to affirm that reality. I kept most of what I imagined and felt to myself because there was no one I felt I could communicate with. I understand now that there was something about my imagination that wasn't being fed by the cultural mythos. In a certain way, I was required to spend more time searching for a cosmological framework to support my imagination.

Neither the religious structure we were raised in nor the surrounding folk culture helped me to explain my inner experiences. Our family life focused almost exclusively on daily routines. In search of some larger cosmology, I found museum and library; they became beloved places to explore what lay beyond the conversations at home and community and even beyond my own time.

Waking up

In waking, I open my eyes to the light, remembering what in night was conceived and in waking is born.

The idea, that waking creates, gives us an opportunity to look at where we are now in the beginning of the day as a beginning of a creative intention for who we are to be by the time night comes. We are in this remarkable adventure of beginning again to recall what "night" has given us that only we can give to the world. We're at the point of beginning to decide how to act on behalf of this creative way of life that the human being is endowed with, to be able to give something to the world that the world does not have.

What does it mean: we are at the point? The quality of the veil is more transparent now in this point of time.

Awaking to the Heart

When I was about six, a teacher asked me a question; I was lost in thought and did not hear her. At first, she thought I was ignoring her. Once she got my attention I watched her carefully. I could see that she was deliberating inwardly about what she should do. In her heart, I saw that she understood that I had been absorbed in contemplation, and that she should let the incident pass. But the "rules" prescribed otherwise. So, after a moment of inner conflict, she punished me.

What struck me forcibly was that she had betrayed her heart. I asked myself—why would she do something her heart was telling her not to do? At that moment I made a vow that I would never betray my heart. Making this vow, I awoke to another level of knowing. I understood that my heart was something to safeguard and to act from. I understood that through the heart there is a way of knowing the truth about reality. We can choose to trust it or not. Then and there I made the commitment to stay true to what the heart knows—to trust my heart.

At this time, I also discovered I could turn my attention wherever I wanted. I could create scenarios and live inside them, using my imagination actively and with purpose. This capacity continued to grow and develop throughout my childhood. This needs a little more clarity. Through using this kind of attention, I learned to experience people's motives more clearly. I saw that many people had a fundamental unwillingness to be open and generous. I realized that this was not how I wanted to be and so I determined that giving would be an important part of my life. I understood that to give was part of my commitment to the heart's path of knowing.

Solitude and Friendship

Very early every day before going to school, I made it my intention to prepare myself for the day. I loved quiet mornings. I would wake early, shower, and go to sit silently in a chair by the window to contemplate things. I would go wherever my attention and imagination would take me. It was part day-dream, part meditation.

It was very important for me to have that quiet time. I wanted to be alone. At the other end of the room, the family was busy, full of laughter and conversation. Everyone asked, "Why is he sitting there by himself?" I learned to be alone in a crowd and to be attentive in the midst of conflict. I noticed that because I practiced this inner discipline at home, my attention at school was sharper and more awake. Learning became easier.

During those early mornings, I was also able to choose my roles consciously. I determined what I wanted to be part of and what I did not want to be part of. I learned that I could determine my boundaries. More than that, I could determine who I wanted to be. I learned, too, the value of "inner space" and "sanctuary" and that I could return to these at any time, that I could take them with me wherever I went. "Sanctuary" and "inner awareness" could be anywhere.

This kind of solitude was also at the heart of my relationship with my best friend Brian. We did not always fill our time with speaking. We would greet each other, and then, perhaps, pass one or two remarks. Mostly we were silent. Neither of us liked to speak. Every day we would walk to and from school without speaking. After school, we would sit together without speaking. Yet we were not alone; we were together, in some kind of communion. Primarily, our silence was filled with the feeling that human beings are essentially good. There was a moral, elevating quality about the silence.

In this silence, Brian and I communicated. We did not engage in the usual conversation about what we imagined as most children would do. There were many questions in my own mind yet somehow when we were silent together I felt as if someone else experienced the world as I did. We imagined in the silence. We trusted each other. There was something spiritual about it. It was how I wanted to be with people, how I chose to be. With Brian, I learned that we could convey a great deal in silence and that we were able to create from the silence. Our friendship held the space for something we both valued. It was where we sought the sacred.

In Brian, I witnessed for the first time someone whose motive was neither to exploit nor to harm. He was someone with whom trust was possible. This was an enormous gift, because through that trust, a kind of peace—the peace of being present—descended on us in our shared communicative silence.

When Brian spoke, his language was quite clear and precise. He was devotional; at that time, he was a deeply committed Jehovah's Witness. I was a Seventh Day Adventist but these concepts didn't come between us. Concepts did not determine what we shared. What we shared was rather a way to feel the presence of truth—a way to authenticate ourselves through thinking in silence together. Out of these experiences arose my first notion of inner development. I noticed that I was learning more about myself and it guided me into more conscious steps.

I now realize that what I experienced as a child was the awareness of the motives of other people and the opportunity to decide what level of freedom I could create for myself. I was conscious of my capacity to give, as an inner agreement with myself as a giver, and as an intention to support what others needed. I cultivated the capacity to give without being asked. I was being prepared to give. I understood that I was responsible to give something of myself in order to remain free, to be true to something that I knew was right for me.

Awaking Love

Our feeling life is in contact with and directly influenced by the world of the ancestors. From the ancestral sphere of life we experience inspiration and an impulse to recall something within us that is connected to that world. One of the goals of the ancestral presence is to awaken both the dream and the love within a person, who then becomes impassioned. Aspirations evolve out of the depths of a person's own heart to declare, "I am awake, I am willing to participate in my own nature and in the world." Awakening the dream reveals a self-conscious, self-sufficient being that is able to put seeds into the Earth with the right meaning so that those seeds can actually grow, replenishing, and revitalizing the Earth. This is a state of one's own possibility, pregnant with potential that becomes actual through the gesture of devotion that is strengthened by the ancestral connection to our life.

Watching a Seed Grow

When I was in the fifth grade, we were assigned a project that had significant consequences for me. We were each given a glass jar in which to observe the germination of a seed. We filled the jar half full of water, placed a strip of paper around the inside of the jar, and planted the seed between the glass and the paper. We were instructed to observe it daily and note the changes. Our responsibility was to provide access to light and to ensure there was enough water in the jar. The water evaporated half an inch a day. Refilling the jar every morning was my first "ritual" commitment. It taught me the significance of ritual.

Over time, the seed absorbed both water and light. As it did so, it grew larger. Finally, it began to germinate. Open to wonder, faithful to what I was seeing, I spent hours watching the changes unfold. This project marked the birth of my capacity to observe. It was the beginning of my understanding of time as well as of the nature and potential of seeing. I learned that time was not empty; it flowed with purpose for it influenced everything. Everything changed from moment to moment. Time is a becoming.

Observation was how I used time. I was seeing into the details of what changes from moment to moment. Observation allowed me to enter and use time as a creative way to be part of an experience and to experience the consciousness of having the experience. It was a magical act and it took self-discipline but I learned that practicing it faithfully, I could enter the now, the eternal. This was a first awakening to the power of intention that must be nurtured in us.

I understood that, like the seed, observation too has to be cultivated. The more observation is cultivated, the more the human seed is cultivated. As water and light germinated the seed in the jar, observing the process initiated a kind of germination or awakening in me. As the seed germinated, I awoke.

Water Is the Solvent of Self-interest

During reflection the psyche is activated and an internal space is created for a free act that supports the dissolving of boundaries within the soul. These free forces allow our giving to be called forth. The process of dissolving is symbolized by the element of water. Water is the solvent of self-interest, allowing us to dissolve the boundaries and to create more freedom to decide for the good. Reflection frees us from the limitations of our own experiences and knowledge, linking us to the ancestral pool where the collective consciousness can then support our individual initiative for seeing into the future state of selfhood and deliberately choosing our path.

Immersion

One of my favorite things to do was walk to the beach. My brothers and my friends went to the beach for recreation, but for me this was a meditative experience, almost like walking toward something sacred. At the edge of the water, culture ended and a new type of mystery unfolded before me. It was a dream space that expanded my mind and imagination. I had a precaution, even a slight fear, about the water, so I generally did not swim.

One day, when I was seven, I went with my brothers to the ocean. I waded waist deep into the water and stood there for a while before deciding to return to the shore. Walking back, I had the sudden sensation of stepping into a void, as if there were a great hole in the ocean floor. The vortex was so strong that, in an instant, I was sucked deep down into the hole, swirling and twisting in the vortex. Almost immediately, light filled the hole—or rather, I experienced that the water turned to light. I remember being able to see the walls of the hole that looked as if they were made of layers of bricks. It was almost like a well. I remember thinking, "That's strange. Why would there be a well here?"

The light was so powerful that it penetrated my body. More strangely still, I found that I could breathe under the water. I wasn't panicked. I was awake, observing everything around me. Gradually, it dawned on me how unusual this experience was. I realized that it was unnatural to be able to breathe under water. I knew that some other force was controlling what was happening. Then I became afraid.

I no longer experienced the water. The hole, in fact, contained no water but was filled with fluid light. Then, gradually, the light faded. I rose to the surface. In a daze, I floated on my back, unable to stand on my own. I was deeply shocked and exhausted by the experience. Someone saw me floating in the shallow water and pulled me to the shore.

The entire experience abruptly disappeared. It was as if I suddenly woke up. I sat on the beach with a throbbing headache. When my brothers appeared, I told them that I had fallen in a hole. They asked: "Did you almost drown?" I said, "No," but something kept me from telling them exactly what had happened. The experience was a secret that I kept to myself. I did not understand it. Years later, it came up in a divination ritual with my friend Malidoma Somé. Only then did I learn of the significance of this day on the beach.

Death and Healing

When I was about nine years old, a friend my age was killed in an automobile accident. This was my first encounter with the death of someone I knew. My friend's sudden absence raised a question in me: What is death? Asking it, I felt suddenly awake, more conscious, and more deeply aware of my own being. I felt impelled to find out about death.

This was a new type of desire to know. I already knew what it was to want to know something that could be found in a book. I was quite an avid researcher, well known at the library. For the first time, what I wanted to know could not be found in books; I knew that it could be found only in experience. Now I understood that I had to find the answer in life.

I had the inner conviction that something as meaningful as my friend's life could not just end. I wanted confirmation of his continued existence. I had been opened to the possibility of something beyond the nature of the body. This was a new feeling. I didn't feel the loss that everyone else expressed. My thinking about my friend's death generated a feeling in me that he was still there. I wanted to attend his funeral to see for myself if I could find a way to stay in touch, in communication.

At the funeral, all the adults were grief-stricken and weeping. I remember thinking, "They don't know how to understand." I approached the coffin and stood there, looking at my friend's face. I was overwhelmed by the stillness of it. I felt as if I were alternately losing and gaining consciousness—almost as if my consciousness were breathing. On the spot, I made an intention to stay connected to him; I wanted to understand the realm of death. I felt that he would be able to help me.

A few months later, my grandmother died of tetanus-septicemia. She had suffered a puncture wound from a nail and, because she did not like hospitals, had refused early medical attention. Three days later, she died. I wondered why she had closed up, shut herself off, and did not seek help. I asked myself whether anything could have been done for her if she had sought help. I wanted to know why human beings were vulnerable to illness and death. Could anything have prevented her dying? What would healing be? Could it prevent dying? Could others be prevented from dying? Was it a matter of timing?

These questions led me to an understanding that human beings have the capacity to protect and guide the physical body. I was using my contemplative process to explore my own physical body. The questions were also an investigation. Where does the energy for healing come from? I used to pay attention to funerals in a very intentional way. Death offered something that was not integrated into our consciousness. It is often not integrated. We could heal in other ways by understanding the realm of the dead. Death had more to tell us about the life of the person and about life itself. I felt that there was an aspect of the spirit that could support healing and transformation of consciousness if we allowed ourselves to know about life behind the reality of death. There was more to the story than other people seemed to recognize; they were trying to make contact but we could not hear them. Through my own processes and experiences, I began to understand the nature of separate realities that a human being can experience. It became clear to me that the physical body carried a much larger power, which an individual could become aware of and that provided other levels of experience that we can guide and control. I had begun to feel that people were dying because they were unaware of the connection between the body and life. Also they did not understand enough about the body and its connection to the life that lives beyond it. Was the soul actually keeping the body alive?

It seemed to me important to be able to prevent illness, to learn to live in a way that prevented illness. I decided to take care of myself in such a way that I would not become ill. At the same time, I realized that death was always present in life—that to live was to experience death around us. I discovered that in living there is a deeper knowledge of death. Life requires that we know something about ourselves and others, and this memory supports a realization that death is not an end. I understood that if I exercised responsibility for life, then I could include death as part of my life.

I saw that my grandmother had never been able to meet life. People and relationships were difficult for her. I realized that the ability to die in a truly human way depended upon the capacity to meet life with openness and a will to engage in relationships.

This awareness came to me at my grandmother's funeral, where I witnessed the community—my family and others—experiencing a loss. I saw that they were unable to make contact with the part of themselves that understood, on a deeper level, what her life meant in relation to ours. They spoke about her as being gone but this was not so for me. As I moved through conversations and encounters after the funeral, deep memories stirred within me. I felt the presence of the ancestors, reaching back to the beginning. I felt a kind of joy in the midst of the grief of my family and the community. For me, the burial became a ritual of creating a sacred space, a shrine dedicated to the remembrance of my grandmother. I understood that, in order to make contact with her, I only had to hold this place where she was laid to rest in my mind. I now had another connection to the ancestral world.

Meeting the Other

While still a high school student in 1982, I immigrated with my family to the United States. Between 1978 and 1982, parts of the family had moved at different times. Parents wanted to create opportunities for us that we would not have in Guyana. We settled in Brooklyn. Living in a new place presented challenges and I sought a community in which to be at home and grow. In Guyana, my community had been given; in the United States it would have to be made. I would have to find or create a community for myself.

I knew that community was a sharing of values and that a person developed spiritually through the community he or she belonged to. I had learned in Guyana that community was a shared way of living, one that inspired people to give and exchange. But where was my place in the United States?

In the school I attended, there was a group of Haitians. They were disliked because they looked different. They were much darker than the other students and, worse still, they spoke another language, which seemed almost pathological to the majority. At the same time, they were much more social than the other students. They formed a kind of school within the school. They had their own classes taught in French. They had a culture and they shared goals. In a way, they still enjoyed a kind of living tribal imagination. Theirs was a culture of deep relationships. Having been brought up in a predominantly European, Anglo environment, I was enormously captivated by their more "African" quality. And so I consciously decided to explore what others denied and were not seeing.

A Haitian classmate spoke English. I asked if I could attend his club meeting. He asked his friends, and they said I could come. When I attended their gathering they asked if I wanted to say something to them. I shared some words of encouragement and I spoke of how human beings can support each other and remain strong, despite being isolated. I spoke to them in English and my words had to be translated. Despite this, I was welcomed. For the first time, I experienced what it is to be a stranger and to be welcomed and unconditionally accepted. From then on, the Haitian students always greeted me in Creole. I found sanctuary in their greeting and their welcome. Though we seldom spoke and we did very little together, I understood I had been seen by this group. A real exchange took place even when we just passed in the corridor or on the street. I felt "seen," witnessed.

Later, I learned the Zulu greeting *sawubona*, meaning "we see you." As noted in chapter 1, in South Africa, when you meet someone, and he or she says "*sawubona*," you reply "*Yebo sawubona*" (we see you, too). Seeing is an agreement. "We see" and "we are seen" are one gesture. This implies that there is a greater presence at play when two human beings come together in shared seeing. *Sawubona* elevates the reality of mutual human acknowledgment by affirming that in human relatedness a greater spiritual reality is present. My Haitian friends gave me my first experience of mutual seeing and recognition. They taught me that to be seen is healing.

Social Impulses

There are two threads that are fundamental to my path. The first is initiation, the process that develops a person's capacities to make the deepest possible connection to the world. As a child, I intuitively experienced initiation through the various episodes already described. I carried a subtle awareness of the world of the dead. This ancestral presence influenced what I understood about the world. Only much later in life did I experience conscious initiation processes under the guidance of elders in Africa.

The second thread is human rights—the question of what the human being is entitled to that supports individual development and social possibilities. The thread of human rights began for me in Guyana when, as a child, I attended the political rallies of Dr. Walter Rodney, a human rights activist, economist, historian and founder of the political party, Working Peoples Alliance. I observed Dr. Rodney's capacity to unite people of different cultural backgrounds in creating common agreements around their political understanding of their rights as people. He was able to build a movement beyond race and class, giving meaning to the economic striving. I was interested in understanding what he was describing as a new possibility for Guyana.

One afternoon in 1980, my cousin, who was a nurse at the hospital in Georgetown, came to our family's home with the news that Dr. Rodney had been injured by a bomb and taken to the hospital, where he died. I remember being tremendously shocked by this news; I had, after all, been present at one of his rallies only a few days earlier. I was angry at this act of violence against someone who had love for a cause, a people, and a country. I needed to understand more fully what had led to his assassination.

Dr. Rodney's assassination opened other levels of violence among the various political groups. At the same time it was a call for people to step fully into their political power. I felt drawn by his death to actively engage in the fundamental right to pursue free thought about the social directions and cultural aims of both individuals and groups. I engaged in my first political protest at the funeral of Dr. Walter Rodney as we marched in a procession through the streets of Georgetown toward the place of his burial. It felt like a march for a cause that reached beyond my understanding but I was compelled to participate. It took courage because of the political atmosphere in which it was happening. It took courage to protest against a government that was responsible for his death. My right to freely act was affirmed by the risk he took to speak for it and to speak for those who were rendered voiceless and powerless by a government that took away freedoms for its own self-gain.

Several years later when I attended college in the United States, I became involved in the antiapartheid movement, which was bringing the South African struggle to light. This political activism was what first brought me toward the spiritual impulses that South Africa holds for the world. While in college my studies focused on the historical context of the struggle on the continent of Africa and in the Diaspora. I was part of a coalition of students and teachers who advocated increasing the availability of African and African-American Studies departments on the college campuses within the state of California.

These experiences provided an important learning framework because they informed us of our civil and political rights as well as the fundamental human principles that support the highest strivings of an individual. They also linked us to a deep historical context that included the Civil Rights

Movement, the cultural art renaissance in Harlem, the Reconstruction Movement, the Abolitionist Movement, the Middle Passage, the colonization of African resources and people, and the pre–Colonial nature of African civilization and the people who sustained these cultural strivings. My education linked me to history. It created a context for future initiatives that arose out of the capacities emerging from civil, cultural, and spiritual development.

Through my study of history, the capacities that I carried within my life became active in reformulating what that history was connected to on its deeper level. I was not investigating dead facts or finished realities. Rather I was discovering a way to communicate with my ancestors, those who had lived these experiences that had shaped their consciousness and their dreams. They communicated to me what I should know in order to affect outcomes to which this history was connected. My present life emerged out of this history. I carry history with me.

We human beings are guided by primal intuitions that support our ideal striving and our moral development. Morality is a memory that flows through us from the highest potential in our soul. When we are able to find methods and procedures to integrate this memory, we pursue goodness, truth, and beauty.

5
GNOSTIC INITIATION

WHAT IS KNOWING?

In the twelfth grade, I had an exceptional teacher, who brought philosophy more consciously into my life. Although technically-speaking she taught English, she sought to ground us in fundamental questions. She introduced us to Greek philosophy and tragedy. I remember a class discussion—we were talking about Socrates—that centered on the concept that if human beings truly know goodness, they will pursue it. I argued that knowing on those deeper levels is possible; if we know the deeper meaning of goodness, we will pursue it. Everyone else argued against me, saying there was no such thing as the good. I felt that goodness was a choice, a decision. The others thought I was being too idealistic and metaphysical.

My understanding both then and now is that goodness is not based on information or knowledge. On other levels goodness can be reached and provide precise insights into "who I am" and "what I can give" as meaning for reality. I was aware that if we don't add something to our motive, then reality appears to be finished. Goodness requires an activation of this level of intention in order to bring an experience to a place where we can say it is good. We can reach goodness if we continue to try to attain a level of consciousness we reach when the motive is clear and precise enough. Attention and intention. Goodness is intentional. It can't be there unless you set a conscious motive for it. It is possible to move the facts of circumstances to intuitive certainty. My thinking supports knowing the nature of reality; there is a level beyond what is already known if I pursue it far enough. The realm of possibility for a higher level of truth always felt attainable to me. The understanding of the good was not in relationship to established standards, but a level of giving of one's free will to something that supports the free expression of others.

At about the same time, I was asked to memorize and recite for an assembly in honor of Black History Month Langston Hughes' poem "Let America Be America Again." The spiritual influences that inspired the poetic mind of the author of these profound words brought into my awareness the underlying contributions of African thought: the emancipated heart and mind and the pioneering spirit for what America was destined to be. The words provided, for me, access to the author's imagination of what lay beyond the given reality. Through this poem Langston Hughes also authored a possible future that can be known by the openness of the heart. The poem leads to the deeper sphere of belief and faith. The poem became my text to a larger understanding of what lay hidden in the collective soul of a people and the spiritual destiny of a nation. It awoke within me a spiritual striving, to find the language and methods of delivery for the ancestral memory that was being awakened.

I felt that the ancestors now wanted to be heard and wanted to speak through these words to support a shared understanding of what was possible through human communication. The prophetic nature of "Let America Be America Again" would remain for me an open door to the inner call, a form of initiation that would make my destiny path clearer. From this point on, I knew that my path had to do with a peculiar history, poetic language: the social, spiritual science that would support the agreements for a land that honors the nobility of soul within each person's destiny. I discovered words and their rhythms. They guide the human mind through the corridors of time—past, present and future. They guide the human mind into the spheres of knowledge created through human experience, the world of nature and the world of cosmic ideas. I became a seeker for the methods of knowing that lay beyond the accepted disciplines of study.

Let America Be America Again

Let America be America again.
Let it be the dream it used to be.
Let it be the pioneer on the plain
Seeking a home where he himself is free.

(*America never was America to me.*)

Let America be the dream the dreamers dreamed—
Let it be that great strong land of love
Where never kings connive nor tyrants scheme
That any man be crushed by one above.

(*It never was America to me.*)

O, let my land be a land where Liberty
Is crowned with no false patriotic wreath,
But opportunity is real, and life is free,
Equality is in the air we breathe.

(*There's never been equality for me,*
Nor freedom in this "homeland of the free.")...

—Langston Hughes

Black Gnosticism

In 1990 I attended a discussion group at the Aquarian Spiritual Center in Los Angeles. The group was facilitated by Dadisi Sanyika, a senior member of the Black Gnostic Studies Program of the center. I recognized him as well as a member of the staff from Charles Drew University of Medicine and Science where I worked. We exchanged greetings and we were, in a way, surprised to be meeting in such a different context. I would come to understand their deeper interests in human spiritual development and the social, scientific study and practice that were the purpose of the school.

Near the end of our session that evening, I noticed an elderly gentleman coming down the stairs to join us. He chose to sit at the back of the class and was attentive to our conversation. He said nothing but imbued a strong presence that increased my interest in knowing who he was. At the end of the class Dadisi told us that he was Dr. Alfred Ligon, the founder of the Aquarian Spiritual Center and the Black Gnostic Studies Program. Dr. Ligon had founded the Aquarian Book Shop in 1941 and introduced the metaphysical disciplines to the African-American communities in Los Angeles. Later he founded the Aquarian Spiritual Center and the University of Occult Philosophy. I learned that Dr. Ligon was a member of the Sabian Assembly and the Brotherhood of Light, both theosophical schools, and that he had studied with Mark Edmund Jones, who had founded the Sabian Assembly.

Dr. Ligon was trained in theosophy and as a metaphysician. He formed a process of study and practice that he called Black Gnosticism—an integration of Egyptian mysticism and

African Gnosis. His intention was to reconstitute the ancient Mystery Traditions into a new discipline of study consisting of the appropriate social understanding for the African-American experience. The tradition of Gnosticism involves exploring knowledge systems; Dr. Ligon considered Black Gnosticism to be about the hidden or inner teachings. He drew from these teachings of the religious and symbolic systems of the Piscean Age, covering a period of the past two thousand years. The twelve Piscean schools can be traced to twelve mystery schools dealing with religious and symbolic systems underlying civilization across these millennia.

The Aquarian Spiritual Center was created to prepare for the Age of Aquarius, the emerging astrological age. The primary purpose of the school was to utilize the Egyptian/African mystery teachings to support the development of present day soul consciousness. Through the curriculum Dr. Ligon introduced the writings of many Eastern and Western traditions. The primary work of the Center was to formulate new methods to investigate the African-American spiritual initiation. The work was also to document the Gnostic tradition consistent in the music, art, and literature of blacks in America. He outlined for us the various personalities that stood as representatives of the Gnostic tradition. Utilizing astrology and other symbolic systems, he explored the significance of the biographies of certain significant personalities that played a role in what he called "group destiny of Black America." These included many cultural leaders, scholars, and activists of the various movements from the Abolitionist period to the Civil Rights era.

I joined Dr. Ligon's school in 1991 and studied with him for thirteen years. He had a twenty-year curriculum and he mentored me through thirteen of those. There was great wisdom in how he related to me and devised my studies along what was called the seventh-ray path, formulated by Alice Bailey's book *The Rays and the Initiations: A Treatise on the Seven Rays* (vol. 5). It is called the path of absolute sonship. The path involves the workings of group karma and group consciousness and creating the social tasks through which a group destiny can be realized. It is also the path of Isis in the process of putting back together the separated parts of Osiris. Dr. Ligon referenced the path for me by integrating the term cosmotherapy or healing through love. The curriculum involves a practice of service to those spiritual beings that are holding the ritual laws for the prophecies that the people possess as potential within themselves. This practice is centered on the rites of ceremonial order and ritual. It involves mental, psychic, and moral disciplines for making contact with the spiritual world. The disciplines of the path of absolute sonship provide an understanding of the soul consciousness of the group that I am culturally connected to in America. It provides the social context for the integration of the African philosophical teachings into a Western social worldview. This became the basis of my practice.

For more than sixty years, Dr. Ligon played a significant role in the lives of many black cultural leaders, artists, and intellectuals. The main branch of his school in Los Angeles was named the Pascal Beverly Randolph Lodge, in recognition of the architect of the Rosicrucian movement in the United States and the cultural avatar for the emancipation of African slaves. Dr. Ligon died in 2002 at age ninety-six. The school remains active through the practitioners, who have chosen a path of service toward the larger unfolding of the spiritual reality of which he made us aware.

Soon after I joined Dadisi's study group at the Aquarian Spiritual Center in South Central, Los Angeles, I was asked to write a personal myth, based on my zodiacal birth sign of Cancer. The following day, I was sitting quietly after morning meditation, thinking about birth as a prophetic process. I thought of birth itself as a particular calling to destiny. As I did so, a spontaneous vision came to me. I began to write down what I was seeing. It was a story about a unique child, born into a nomadic community under an astronomical configuration that heralded a special birth, occurring only once in every three hundred years.

In the story, a male child born in this way was given the name "grandfather," while a female child was called "grandmother." The title indicated that the child was the holder of a prophecy, a deep ancestral memory that spanned many generations. This child was the seventh birth in a cycle of births occurring every three hundred years, culminating in a 2,100-year cycle, or an astronomical age. Each child represented an essential wisdom teaching that was to be brought to the community. It was the task of each of these individuals to fulfill the prophecy of erecting the shrines that symbolically represented this wisdom.

My story told of how this seventh child came to initiate the seventh shrine. I did not know precisely what the seventh shrine was. Two weeks after the child was born, spiritual beings came and took the child into the spiritual world. During this period, he was schooled by ancestral beings in the mysteries he would bring to his people. When he was fourteen, he was returned to the community to share what he had learned of the seventh shrine, which the community was charged to create.

That was it. My vision ended abruptly with the community setting off on a journey toward the place where the shrine was to be created. I had no idea what they would find. I wrote out of meditation and, when the inspiration dried up, I stopped. It would be several years before this vision would be explained to me through an African elder.

Meeting Anthroposophy

In 1994 I was working as a research fellow at the Center for the Study of Violence and Social Change under the directorship of Dr. C. Boyd James, social scientist and historian, and Dr. Lewis King, psychiatrist and cultural theoretician. The Center was part of the Frantz Fanon Research Institute at Drew University. I was invited to join the research team of the Center to pursue the development of intervention models for healing individuals and communities exposed to a high incidence of violence. Our primary aim was to explore the resiliency of the individuals and groups affected by the historical exposure to social and political violence over extended periods of time.

A large segment of our work followed the research and writings of Dr. Frantz Fanon, who was a psychiatrist and primary architect of social strategies for the recovery from posttraumatic stress inherited through generational exposure to violence. Through this work we were introduced to communities in Los Angeles where there was a high incidence of gang violence. These included the city of Englewood, the city of Compton, South Central Los Angeles and the community of Watts.

Around this time, two friends introduced me to Tim Smith, a professor of geography at Cal State, Dominguez Hills. Tim was very interested in the spiritual dimensions of life that serve human development. We planned to meet for conversation at Tim's home. That evening I drove to Grenada Hills, where Tim and his wife Eva met us. I learned that they were part of the Anthroposophic community in Los Angeles and that they also worked at Highland Hall Waldorf School. It was the first time I heard the name of Rudolf Steiner in the context of a whole body of knowledge. I was intrigued.

That evening led to further conversations with Tim and Eva about my interest in early childhood development. My work involved the creation of healing processes for children that are exposed to violence. They introduced me to two teachers at Highland Hall. We started a study group on Waldorf pedagogy and healing. I was impressed with Steiner's clear, cognitive picture of human development and with a pedagogical process that was clearer than any I had previously encountered.

Tim was preparing to go to an Anthroposophic conference in Sacramento and he invited me to come along. I learned it was a conference celebrating the hundredth anniversary of Steiner's major philosophical work, *The Philosophy of Freedom*, which clearly explains the presence of the spiritual world in each person. It outlines a philosophy of direct cognitive participation in various realms of the cosmos as well as consciousness in man. It presents a total picture of the progression of conscious thought, feelings, and actions directed to the realm of the spirit.

The first person I met at the conference was Dennis Klocek, author of *Seeking Spirit Vision*. He greeted me saying,

"Welcome, brother." It was a moment of fellowship, of kinship. I felt somehow I had returned and that I was home. Dennis's lecture opened up a new way of thinking for me that I sensed could provide a framework for all I was doing. Richard Tarnas spoke on his book *The Passion of the Western Mind*. Robert McDermott spoke on Rudolf Steiner. Friedemann Schwarzkopf spoke on steps to meditation drawn from Steiner's *Philosophy of Freedom*. The discussion went beyond any concept I had previously encountered on the activity of the human mind and spirit. I felt that here was thinking that reflected my own imagination and aspirations. At the end of the evening I decided to attend Friedemann's workshop the following day.

During the workshop I made some remarks. Friedemann leaned forward, listening intently. When I finished, he was silent. I wondered if what I said had been off the point. I later spoke a second time. Again Friedemann was silent. Feeling unsure, I decided to say no more and just observe. Later, after the workshop, I was walking toward the campus when I heard a voice calling me. It was Friedemann. He came up to me and thanked me for what I had shared. He said there were two moments when the Holy Spirit entered the room and those were the two moments when I had spoken. He offered me a book that he was carrying. It was entitled *Thinking–Feeling*, a collection of essays he had translated for Georg Kühlewind. He said that there were two essays in particular that he thought were meant for me. This encounter marked the beginning of a remarkable period of growth and learning in my life.

Friedemann and I talked on the phone periodically over the next few months. He invited me to his home in Colfax for his wife's birthday and I went. More conversations followed. He gave me a copy of *Metamorphosis of the Given*, his dissertation. He followed up with a long handwritten letter outlining methods to use in studying the book. He suggested a different order of chapters from what was given. Back in Los Angeles, I told Tim and Eva about it. They got copies of the book and we decided to extend our study group to work on this book. Two others joined us; we studied the book for two years.

This work was a profound initiation experience for me. We focused on the practice of dissolving the given, which Friedemann defined as everything that appears in sense perception and cognition to which we give attention. Through these exercises, I was able to reconnect with very early meditative and cognitive experiences and give them a conscious form. I was introduced to a method of cognition that leads to better understanding the nature of reality and the possibility for shared awareness between two or more human beings.

My interest in healing was expanded by the practice that was introduced in *Metamorphosis of the Given*. The text outlined methodologies for understanding what we as human beings do through the attentiveness that creates reality. The nature of reality as such begins when we are attentive to the inner experiences that a human being creates and that give structure to the outer forms we identify as reality.

Friedemann taught that thinking is a creative act. It allows the human being to observe a world that begins with the human process of intention and attention. Human consciousness facilitates the co-creation of the worlds of understanding and truth, allowing the spiritual world to be experienced in the stages of what becomes reality. This phenomenon of consciousness remains largely hidden but it can be observed through meditative or conscious attention. This requires making conscious the very activity that we normally engage in unconsciously, the giving of attention. When we are able to observe our intentional activity and concentrate its influence we can participate in healing, the recovery of the lost forces that sustain and renew the nature in which we participate. Attentiveness heals.

Friedemann and I met every few months for some years. We talked about our work. One day he invited me to a meditation retreat with Georg Kühlewind in New Mexico. This turned out to be another provocative learning experience. At the heart of the workshop was the idea of the power of the word—the Logos. Kühlewind explored how the written word holds the dynamics, the power of the spirit, and the power of meaning. He described how communication is itself a door through which meaning flows into understanding, leading to the cultivation of a higher consciousness that itself becomes a grace in the world. Here the understanding of beginning—the predisposition of the Logos to begin—made its most powerful impact on my life. It made a significant contribution to the body of work I had initiated called "The Genesis Pathway," a cognitive therapeutic process of mentoring the spirit of an individual to decide for a future.

6

THE STORY OF LAZAR

What Is The Story?

The story is our way of remembering and, in a sense, putting back together the archetypal forces of the soul. It's a way of constructing the archetypal frameworks for the activities going on in the inner regions of human life consciousness. The story frames our realizations and dreams and through our contemplation of it helps to mature our thinking to its own ideal level. It is the ancient way of giving birth to the thinking life, helping it orient itself toward the symbolic as well as the real. It teaches us how to listen in to ourselves and to hear the voice that calls us into faith: a preparation for the future that we are going to live. The story includes levels of the ideal, the real, the symbolic, and the specific nature of human potential.

I Meet Lazar

As I often did, one Thursday during the summer of 1989 I went to a jazz club in Leimert Park Village with some friends. Leimert Park Village in Los Angeles is a cultural center for African Americans. It is a lively spot, bubbling over with poetry slams, music, dancing, and drumming.

As I was leaving the club, a tall man appeared as if out of nowhere and approached me from behind. He must have been about twenty-one and had a bounce to his walk. He called after me, "I have a favor to ask." I turned to see who it was. As if we knew each other, he asked, "Can I borrow ten dollars?" I looked at him with surprise. He explained, "I need it for gas. I'll pay you back." I hesitated. It seemed so abrupt, without any introduction or preparation.

I recognized that the word *borrow* meant that we would have to meet again. Could I trust him? He must have read my thoughts, for he said innocently, "I'll make sure I get it back to you." I gave him the money, and he thanked me. He said that he was an artist and that he would like me to see his work. Then, before he left, he insisted on giving me his name—Lazar McDaniels—and his telephone number. I did not think I would see him again.

For several days, I kept wondering whether this strange person could be trusted. There was something unsettling about the whole experience. It stayed in my mind. I wanted to understand the truth in the encounter. Was there a possibility of his keeping his word? Finally, about a week later, I called the number he had given me. I wasn't sure whether it was valid, but it was. Lazar answered. I recognized his voice immediately. For a moment, I was shocked. I felt guilty about my lack of trust. As we talked, suspicions disappeared. Lazar told me to come over the next day at 3:30 in the afternoon and gave me directions to a house in Pasadena.

My brother drove me to the address I had been given. It was a gated community. I pressed the bell to his apartment, but there was no answer. We waited for about half an hour and were about to leave when a young woman, who I later learned was his girlfriend, came to the gate. I asked her about

Lazar. Did he actually live there? She said he did, but that he was always late. We talked a while. I gave her my telephone number and asked her to give it to Lazar when she saw him. Then my brother and I left. That evening, Lazar called and he was full of apologies. He asked me whether I could come again, and we made an appointment for the next day.

I arrived on time and he was there. Opening the door, he seemed in a great hurry. He said he had to leave immediately. "You wait here," he added. "I have to pay a bill, I'll be right back." And suddenly I found myself alone in this strange person's apartment. Who was this chaotic individual? I sat down. The place was filled with evergreen plants, Chinese lanterns, and bamboo torches. There were beautiful paintings on the walls. In the middle of the room stood a half-broken glass-topped coffee table, with grass that had been intentionally planted to grow through the opening. There was also an aquarium with a lizard in it.

A half an hour later, Lazar returned—with pizzas, soda, and more profuse apologies. We had hardly sat down before he jumped up, saying, "I have something I want to show you." He opened the back veranda door to reveal a large foam sculpture of a head. The size and detail were impressive. He explained that it was part of a float he was preparing for the Pasadena Tournament of Roses Parade. I later learned that he was a professional float builder, the youngest builder for the parade.

Lazar overflowed with imagination as he told me what his float would look like when complete. He talked and talked. His enthusiasm carried both of us away. Filled with joy and excitement, he described all that he planned to do. His artistry was palpable. I listened raptly, and that is how our friendship began.

Over the next two years, we talked frequently on the phone and saw each other every two weeks or so. We spoke about art and business, and our lives. Lazar was forming a company and wanted me to become involved. I introduced him to other artists and, gradually, he became a real friend. At the same time, he always remained something of a mystery. He was very solitary, introverted, and private. He guarded his solitude and kept himself to himself. He was unable to socialize—he told me his childhood had been difficult and had left him wounded. If contact was not required for a work-related matter, he would avoid people whenever he could. He was uncomfortable within himself. He thought of himself as "ugly," yet I sensed a "great" soul—innocent, naive, creative. I was hopeful that one day he would truly be seen for what he could do.

Lazar Comes to Stay

One day in spring, several years after I had first met Lazar, I returned from medical school to my apartment in Los Angeles. The building manager, Nigel, an artist to whom I had introduced Lazar, informed me that Lazar was waiting for me in Nigel's apartment. I went upstairs. A few minutes later, Lazar appeared at my door. He told me he needed a place to stay. He explained that he owed ten thousand dollars for drugs, and the dealers were after him. I was shocked, but without hesitating, invited him to stay with me. He promised he would try to get help for his drug problems. That evening, Nigel, Lazar, and I talked about what help he would need.

For me, it was the end of the semester, and I had to go to New York to visit with family. I left Lazar in my apartment. When I returned, I could see he was ill. He had difficulty breathing and was very weak. I asked him how long he had been in this condition. "Only a couple of days," he said. He was running a fever and thought he had flu. I went out to get him some over-the-counter flu medication, but he did not improve. That night, he had night sweats, and I knew it was serious.

The next morning, I took him to the emergency room at Martin Luther King Jr. Community Hospital. He had to be admitted, so I left him there and went home. That evening, a doctor called to speak with me. They wanted to do an HIV test, but Lazar would not give them permission to do so. He had told them to ask my opinion, so I asked to be connected to Lazar. We talked and he agreed to have the test.

I returned to the hospital the next morning ad Lazar was released. He was still very weak and slept most of the time. I felt the weight of something very complicated, something that would make huge demands of me, entering my life. In fact, it would last three years. For three years, slowly but gradually, Lazar would deteriorate.

Three days after his test, we went back to the hospital to hear the results. Lazar went in to see the doctor alone. Two hours later he emerged, crying. He walked straight up to me, made direct eye contact, and asked, "Am I going to die?" I was speechless, shocked. I knew what it meant, but could not answer. I was thinking, "How is he going to live with this? What can I do for him now?" I knew he had nowhere else to turn—that I was the only help he had.

I had taken the day off from work. We drove to the Self-Realization Fellowship headquarters in Pacific Palisades. There are beautiful gardens there, overlooking a pond. Close to a statue of Gandhi, we sat and talked. It was my first real glimpse into the complexity of Lazar's life, his tragedies and losses. I learned of his abandonment by his father and his tortured, almost pathological, but deep, love-filled relationship with his mother. For both of us, it was an initiation conversation. We had true *indaba*, or deep talk. Lazar began to teach me how to be present to another human being whose life is hanging by a thread.

It was the first such conversation of many. He revealed that what he really needed was trust—trust to be able to share, to communicate, to be understood. We talked until the sun set. Then we went home. I knew my question, my task, was: how to support him in every possible way. Thus began a life ruled by demanding medical needs. There were frequent trips to the hospital, plus the close monitoring of his medication and nutrition.

Whenever Lazar recovered enough, he went back to work, to create something for himself. His last work would be a float depicting Martin Luther King Jr. Meanwhile, my family and friends could not understand why I would choose to live with someone with AIDS. They were afraid. But I could not violate the sacred trust that Lazar had conferred upon me. I would find him the help he needed.

Our deep conversation continued. My work at medical school began to fall apart. Lazar became my true work. Our friend Nigel was a great help during crises, and our working together seemed to bring additional support to Lazar. I began to understand something of the spiritual dynamics of community, where two or more are gathered together for the sake of something greater. Lazar was the heart, the mystery at the center of our work. I felt his life calling me to enter it. I began to listen as intently as I could to what his heart spoke—to try to understand what the future could be for him and where I fit into its unfolding.

Throughout the experience of working with Lazar, I had a sense that a promise was being made not so much by him or by me individually, but as a result of our sharing, our being together. This promise kept me going, even though its specific nature was unknown. I knew in the deepest way. This knowledge kept growing in conviction—that something was coming toward us from the future. Providing care for Lazar was the hardest thing I had ever had to do. Yet the promise was that something important would come out of the experience. My faith in that promise carried me through the difficult days and the constant uncertainty.

My task was to make his burden light. This meant ensuring, twenty-four hours a day, that he did not feel abandoned. This, in turn, meant continually protecting, confirming, and enhancing the trust that he had invested in me. This trust was tested, over and over again, because Lazar would repeatedly relapse into drug use. He would have to go into rehab and then once he recovered, would relapse again and once again return to rehab—and so on and on.

During this period, I began to understand the power of love—how it moves between human lives. I understood, too, that when one is connected to love in this way, sacrifice is inevitable. Mostly, I just listened. I did not ask questions. I would just accept what I was given. Somehow, I knew that in such circumstances human truth does not come from questioning. Experience taught me that too often questions only elicit lies, evasions, and denials. I had to learn to rely on faith that what I needed to know would emerge when I needed to know it, by grace. I knew I was carrying out a spiritual obligation. I began to ask myself how much of the past really matters. I realized one could only listen. One cannot "figure out" another person's life. I never did discover how Lazar had contracted AIDS.

Often, we read and talked about the Bible, mostly the New Testament and Psalms. Somehow, in Lazar's mind, this process was part of his recovery. He wanted to prepare for his death. He did not know the Bible and asked me to teach him about it. Together, we would pick what he wanted to read. We spoke a lot about the Resurrection, about life and death, and the nature of the Christ. He tried to understand the meaning of Christ's sacrifice. As we talked, insights flowed to us. There were times when we felt connected to a reality that was larger than ourselves. Our understanding became clearer about a future that Christ had prepared, that the Resurrection had prepared. Together, we stood in the Mysteries and shared our faith. Together, we came to understand that forgiveness is the heart of love—that love and forgiveness are inseparable. This helped Lazar overcome the great breaches that he felt separated him from his family. Slowly, he was able to forgive all the loved ones who had wounded him so deeply. He was able to let go of all that came between him and them.

The Death of Lazar

Looking back, I think of the period with Lazar as the time when I learned the meaning of discipleship to the inner power of love and what we know and call the Christ. Throughout the process, the promise gradually came to me that redemption is revealed not only in life, but also in and after death. Lazar, after death, became more alive and present to me than in life. And through Lazar's own death and rising, Christ, too, became alive for me in a new way.

As time went on, it became clear that Lazar did not really have the will to live. He would not fight to stay alive. Yet, when on the first year of the journey, after he had been in rehab for the first time, his mother became ill and was hospitalized, Lazar left the rehab program and went to stay with her. She had cancer and needed help. Lazar offered help to her, but never told her that he, too, was ill.

One day, he asked me to visit them in Pasadena. His mother opened the door and invited me in. Later, Lazar told me I was the first person his mother had ever invited into her house. He felt that her inviting me, overcoming her fear and lack of trust, demonstrated a kind of unconditional approval. We talked together for about an hour. As I was leaving, she came to the door, and called after me, "I want you to be my son's friend. He will need you."

Lazar stayed with her until she died. When she died, he called me and asked me to come. He had called no one else. When I arrived, he was in the bedroom. It was a small room. He was alone with her body, which lay on the bed. The window was open, and outside one could see his mother's flower garden. Lazar had brought in flowers—pink and white roses—and put them in a vase by her bed. We sat on either side and talked in low tones about her life, about who she was, about their troubled relationship, about what he knew of her story—how she had grown up in Mississippi, how his father had left, abandoning the family, and how she had moved to California. There were long silences. Lazar looked at me across the body. He was weeping. He held her hand and as he did so he was letting her go. He was forgiving her. He looked at her face, and his face was at peace. It was the deepest time that we'd had together—the only time he could truly be himself—and I was the witness. He did not want to be alone in this experience. He wanted someone to witness the release of the conflict and pain he had carried for her.

I said little, but I remembered my grandmother's death. We never left the bedroom. We were held by the deep presence of grief. An amazing lightness filled the room. There was sorrow and at the same time a sense of release. Death held us and let us go. Death was light, not heavy. Then Lazar called the hospital and his sister and the undertaker. He seemed prepared. He was with his mother when she died and it was an easy death. For me, it was the first time I had sat with a body.

We went out into the garden. His sister arrived and the undertaker came and took the body away. Lazar went back up to the bedroom and made up his mother's bed. He changed the sheets because he was still caring for her. Then we went back into the garden. All the relatives were coming. He told me he would be coming back to my house when it was over. His sister would be in charge now. He had done his part. He wanted to stay a few more days to put his mother's things in order. But then he would return to live with me. I realized, then, that my availability to him was going to have to be limitless and unconditional. His mother's death had made it so. She had left him, as he understood it, in a world by himself. She had been his connection to a sense of safety and family. Without her, his understanding was that he was going to be alone. Her death, however, had prepared for him a freedom to embrace his own. I kept returning to her words, "I want you to be my son's friend. He will need you."

In retrospect, Lazar's decision to go home, to look after his mother, seems part of his reconciliation, his path of forgiveness—of coming to terms with his life. He wanted to learn about death without the fear of being alone. He called me because he wanted to see whether I would face death with him. It would give him an idea of how I would act when he, himself, died. He had already made the decision that he would entrust his death to me. I was the one who was left with him. I was the vital connection to what he had still to live out.

His mother's death, which we had shared, was the turning point in his preparation. Through it, he came to accept his own death. Death became the bridge between us as we embarked on a new phase of our mutual transformation. We now had shared memories so profound that they could function as a vessel of inspiration and support a deep trust in the unknown.

After the funeral, which was in the Community Church in Pasadena, where he had been baptized, Lazar returned to my apartment. He stayed for a few months. Then he relapsed into drugs, but once again turned himself around and returned to rehab. I did not know how to deal with his addiction.

One night, he called me from Hollywood. He was high. I had just returned from school. It was about 11:00 p.m. and I was studying. He wanted a ride. I was dead tired, but I had to go. When I picked him up, he smelled strongly of crack cocaine. We did not speak, but drove in silence for a while. He wanted to go to Pasadena to pick up some clothing from his niece. When we got to her house, I parked outside and turned off the engine. We sat next to each other, thinking our own thoughts. He turned to me with teary eyes, filled with gratitude. They seemed to say that everything would be all right—even though he had no will. Wordlessly, he leaned over and put his head on my shoulder. He was asking me for something. I understood what it was—forgiveness. He got out of the car to get the bag his niece had packed for him.

On the way back, he said he would return to rehab. This would be his third attempt—a six-month program. He completed the program and I attended his graduation. He had lost a lot of weight, but it seemed he had broken through to something because he entered a halfway house. He did not like it, but it was part of the program, and he endured it. As he did so, he began to reconnect with his work. He wanted to paint again and started a series of paintings. He gave me one of his mother with butterflies emerging from her hair. In all, he created twelve brightly colored oil paintings and three sculptures, which were exhibited at Claremont College.

After the show, he became very ill. He was weak and lost weight. His vitality seemed to be withdrawing, and then he went into the hospital. After two months, he was moved to hospice. At first, I visited him every day; then, every two or three days. Gradually I could see from his eyes that he was beginning to look into the spiritual world.

One day, toward the end, he asked for a tissue. I rose and went over to the box and brought one back for him. He asked me to wet it. I went over to the sink, soaked it a little, and returned it to him. I sat down on his right side. His eyes were closed. He reached up with his right hand and began to make the gesture of drying someone's eyes. It was as if someone sat on the bed between us. Then he said, "Mom, you remember Orland? I want you to continue to help him and when I come there, I'll help you."

Tears came to my eyes because it was all so real. That was part of the promise. Help from the other side was becoming visible. Lazar could feel the presence of those on the other side and he knew what would be his role there. My listening deepened and once again I began to visit Lazar daily.

One day I arrived and entered his room. Lazar seemed to be asleep. He stirred. My presence appeared to waken him, but he did not open his eyes. I was trying to decide what to do when he suddenly said, "You had better do what you have to do."

"What?" I said.

He said, "You heard me."

Then he repeated, more forcefully, almost like a command: "You had better do what you are here to do."

"What am I here to do?" I asked.

"Don't play games with me," he said. "You know what you're here to do. And if you don't do it, you'll regret it."

What he said was clear. It could not be debated. It was bold and intentional. Lazar was talking about my life and speaking very directly. The veil was removed from my eyes; memories streamed to me from previous experiences in my life, including the immersion in the water when I was seven years old. I felt connected to the ancestral world. Their thoughts flowed to me, and I was thrown into the well again. It was a second initiation. I found a chair and sat down close to the bed. Lazar's eyes were still closed and I tried to remember what I was here to do. I felt a great weight upon me.

Suddenly, Lazar opened his eyes. I struggled to recover myself. As I did so, Lazar turned toward me and reached for my hand. Holding it, he said, "If you go back to medical school, they will not let you become who you are supposed to become. They don't understand the kind of doctor you are supposed to be."

Lazar died January 22, 1995. My last conversation with him was on Christmas Day, December 25, 1994. We had been talking about the Native Americans' animal medicine cards. Lazar had wanted to hear the story of the crow that could not discern things, but would eat everything it saw. Crow was greedy and unconscious. Crow could not choose what was good for him. One day, crow was standing by a lake. Looking out upon the lake, he saw his shadow. The shadow leapt out of the lake and ate the crow. "If I had known that story," Lazar had said, "I would not be lying here."

Turning Point

After Lazar's death, I reflected upon the moment when he had been diagnosed with HIV-AIDS, when he had come out of the conference room with the physician and looked to me, crying, and had asked, "Am I going to die?" In response to that question I had engaged in a conversation with him that resulted in the understanding that, "It doesn't matter if your life is one day, ten years, twenty years—if you can find meaning for it, you will be able to bring into the world the fullness of your own being and feel inwardly self-sufficient and even deeply grateful to have had one day in the world."

This conversation had lasted about three years, from the time he was diagnosed to when he actually died. Not only did it change his life; it also changed mine. It changed my life when he said, "Don't play games with me. You know what you're here to do. If you don't do it, you'll regret it." I had to contemplate what it was that I was here to do. I pulled up a chair next to his bed while he was still sleeping and sat there with the most concentrated intention that I could bring about, trying to remember what it was I was here to do. As I did so, my whole awareness changed. I was able to witness in a new way my ability to establish a conversation with Lazar. This conversation had brought us to an agreement on another level of life. We had come from different directions of life—and death. We had come to this agreement as to the task that we both held: the task in preparing what was a threshold of initiation.

The Veil between the worlds was being removed. I felt myself being seen by the ancestors, who witnessed the service that I had entered to prepare Lazar to enter their worlds. They revealed to me their presence and reminded me of the covenant and the agreements into which I had been born and the work that would unfold in my life through what I had now come to know—how to ask of the ancestors for their help. It was not about who I am in the world as a member of a profession or in a career, but who I am in the world as a human being. I am here to be, in a more fundamental sense, a human being. So when Lazar opened his eyes after a while, we were able to sit in silence witnessing an agreement that allowed us to understand that even if he were not in the body, there would still be a way to communicate.

The agreement is that, as human beings, we're part of the unity of all things. This experience expanded my awareness and broadened the scope of my life and work. Lazar died and I was reborn—born into a conscious intention to live out my life as if this moment is all that I have. I don't want more—of time; I don't want more of anything but what lives in me, and to be able to share that with others who are striving to live as well.

Sanctuary

Sanctuary is a safe, secure place of rest and recovery, a place of shared respect for the conflict a person is in and the potential for change and transformation. It is a place where giving is intentional and cathartic and makes possible the question, "What if?"

Sanctuary is a place of divination where the seeds of possibility are seen. It is a place of help and a place to assess the help that is needed.

Sanctuary is a place where the inner dream is nourished and the inner voice of the call can be heard. It is a place of protection against the constant intrusion of violence and abandonment—a place of peace.

Sanctuary is a place of communication—inner and outer—where the deepest exchange is love. It is friendship, relationship—a home.

Sanctuary is a place of risk, of dynamic tension—between the past and the future, between fate and destiny—where one can search for the right. It is a place to know one another in the light of change and where one can face the consequences of one's life.

Sanctuary is a place outside time, where there is always time for what is needed, a place of practical, continuous support. It is the authentic ground where every individual is welcomed, touched, and cared for.

It is a place of beginning, of faith, healing, forgiveness, imagination, and intention. It is a place of memory, of what lives beyond the temporal.

Sanctuary is a place of initiation where human beings and spirits come together.

It is a place where aspiration and purpose meet. It is a source of the waters of life, a place of reconciliation and resolve, a place of The Word, of the vital exchange of ideas.

Sanctuary is a place of meeting, of mentoring, a place of welcome.

7
RITUAL AND THE RITES OF PASSAGE

Mosaic

In 1991, my friend Dadisi Sanyika invited me to a men's conference that was being sponsored by the Mosaic Multicultural Foundation. Dadisi had been invited by Michael Meade, the founder of Mosaic, to attend the conference and he wanted me to be part of this experience as well. The conference was held in the Malibu Hills at a place called Camp Shalom. It was an annual retreat for men, facilitated by several teachers dedicated to the work of healing men and creating community. Michael Meade, mythologist and storyteller; James Hillman, Jungian psychologist and author; Malidoma Somé, African Elder, teacher, and author; and the poet Robert Bly all offered teachings at the conference that year. There were a little more than a hundred men attending, and by design they were from diverse cultural backgrounds.

For five days, we journeyed into conversations of the soul, the psyche, and culture through storytelling, mythology, depth psychology, and ritual. For all of us, it was a new form of learning, healing, and creating community. I witnessed that within the five days a dynamic and radical change occurred among all of us who shared this experience. We had come from different backgrounds and different points of view and in this event we arrived at the forming of a community.

Among the teachers at this retreat was a remarkable storyteller, someone who had the capacity to reveal through words the images of ancient time and make them relevant to current experience. He did this with the rhythm of drums and a complete willingness to be the bearer of these ancestral messages. Michael Meade knows how to bring into our time messages for the psyche that support the healing of individuals and the making of community. I remember vividly my conversations with him during this event. I recognized in him a friend and a teacher of the understanding of hidden aspects of the human soul that can be awakened through stories and myth, poetry and songs. He saw the edge where we meet with spirits and could formulate methods to cross that threshold.

Michael invited me into a relationship of mentorship that has nourished my life and work ever since, and has guided the evolution and nurturing of the collective community that emerged from this event. He would play a vital role in the rite of passage for many of the young men who came into mentorship through the subsequent founding of Shade Tree Multicultural Foundation.

After the first day of this retreat, Malidoma Patrice Somé from West Africa approached me. We introduced ourselves, and he reflected on things that I had shared during the day. He spoke of his own insights into the experience I was having. Then he made a statement, "You spoke from your belly." I asked him what he meant by that, and he said, "It's a place from which the ancestors speak." With this conversation began our long-standing relationship and our work together with the ancestors and the world of spirit. It opened up the questions that I now wanted to ask. The primary question being

"How can I access the ancestral world and find a cosmology for understanding my path and my work within the community?" He would later share with me his autobiographical book *Of Water and the Spirit*, inviting me to learn more about his path of initiation, the Dagara cosmology, and ritual healing and creation of community.

Malidoma Somé is an elder and a wisdom holder of the Dagara people from the village of Dano in the country of Burkina Faso in West Africa. He brings to the West the teachings of this African tradition of ritual healing and connecting to the worlds of the ancestors. He holds responsibility for certain shrines of the ancestors, specifically, to work with them in the West in order to build relationships with those who have lost their ancestral connection and their connection to the world of nature. His name means "be friends with the stranger/enemy." It is his destiny to bring to the West the rituals and teachings that support people of every ethnicity to understand their ancestral connections.

Malidoma lives in two worlds, including a world shaped by ritual and profound spiritual continuity with the archetypes behind the creation of nature, the cosmology that informs the deeper roots of culture, and the symbolic systems that inform radical initiation. In the West, he also stands as a teacher of the literature of social struggle and pathways for creating community. He continues to play an active role in the shaping of my own initiatory path in relation to African traditional systems. Malidoma is a diviner and helps in the translation of my own cosmological story. He is a bridge to the teachings that inform how I put together and work with the memories that come to me from the world of the ancestors.

As my friendship with Malidoma deepened, I learned from him the experiential presence of other worlds and the purpose of ritual. On one occasion, I visited him at his home at the time in Oakland, California, where his sister Martine was visiting from Burkina Faso. She is a Kontomblé priestess. *Kontomblé* are spiritual beings, allies, concerned with our world and our wellbeing and our relationship with the ancestors. Malidoma and Martine prepared a ritual and invited me to be a part of it. While Malidoma and I waited, Martine went into another room, the shrine room, and made the invocation, a process of opening the ritual space and inviting in the Kontomblé for the purpose of divination. That is, an investigation into the sacred and into the deeper knowledge shared between the physical and spiritual worlds.

As we sat, we heard the invocation and the shaking of a rattle and bell. A Kontomblé entered our realm and began communicating through Martine. Malidoma translated: "They are greeting you, asking how you are and how is your family?" I responded that I was well and that everyone was doing fine. Martine told me that they were glad I was there and that they had a message from the Other World for me. They told me I would play a special role in my family life because of the medicine I carry. Then they said my grandfather had pulled me into the well. I couldn't make sense of this statement. I had never met any of my grandfathers. I was taking what was being said literally. So I responded, "This couldn't be so. I have not met a grandfather." The Kontomblé replied, "This was your grandfather from five generations back, who pulled you into the well to pass medicine on to you. You were the first of those born in your family to whom the gift could be given." They said I would come to know what this medicine was.

I began to remember the experience from when I was a child, the images of being under the water and the presence of light. My senses were opened up again to a level where I was able to recall specific details of what had happened. I knew immediately what they were talking about. Suddenly, everything I had experienced in the hole came back to me. I remembered it all in a flash, as if it had happened yesterday. The Kontomblé allowed me to see what had happened, and in one moment, all the details of the experience became real for me again. I also realized that the Kontomblé spirits had accompanied me since childhood. I understood that through their way of communicating that I had received similar insights. They revealed that they had always been active in my life.

The water medicine, I later learned, is the medicine of reconciliation and return. The waters of light are the waters of forgiveness and transformation. Later, I also found out that this grandfather five generations back had been a water priest. He would take people to the ocean to create rituals. In the ocean, he would open the portals for the waters of light and would perform the ritual submersion of people into them. It was a traditional African form of baptism: through the element of water, taking people completely out of all psychic influences. As a result, they would emerge reconciled with what had been happening to them. Since my grandfather's death, this particular ritual had not been done within the family until my childhood experience of it.

What I learned from the Kontomblé was the importance of ritual; I was a water person, connected through my ancestors to the teachings of the water shrine. The seeds of this knowledge had been sown that day through my immersion in the ancestral pool. After encountering the Kontomblé, I returned again and again in my heart to my experience in the well. As I meditated on it, my question was, "What is the source of the kind of power that can change nature so that a person can breathe under water?"

The ritual experience with the Kontomblé taught me how to recall experiences that had occurred in my life. This ritual taught me to reflect on these experiences in the context of ritual. It taught me to apply African elemental cosmologies to interpret these experiences.

Ritual

Ritual cultivates our devotion to attend to the symbolic, the part of the psyche that dreams. Ritual aspires for contact beyond the daily spheres of human social process. Ritual offers a doorway to the imaginal realms, to the realms of possibility where we revive the inner light of attention and intention. Ritual restores the human contact with the worlds of spirit, nature, and deep culture. It is how we remember what we carry within ourselves that often becomes overshadowed by cultural ambitions. Cultural ambitions place our life outside of its true context. When ritual is carried out with an intention of service to the realms of the ancestors, it is a pathway to the sacred. Through it, we provide ourselves as hosts for the sacred. It occurs when we place deeper questions before ourselves and remain open. Ritual serves as a way to seek help, healing, and knowledge when we are ready to change.

There are different levels of rituals that are integral to the total life of a person or community. They are always present, from the mundane level to the deeper level of the sacred. The mundane level of ritual is where we attend to daily processes that support everyday needs and provide continuity in common social activities, in work or family life—such as preparing meals and attending to the routines of day-to-day life. Ritual can bring healing when something is out of balance, broken, lost, or forgotten; ritual can enable us to reconnect to, revitalize, and replenish strength for optimum wellbeing. Ritual helps as well to acknowledge a beginning such as birth; it provides a way to welcome into the world a new relationship as in marriage or a departure into the ancestral world through death. These latter instances are considered the deeper sacred or "radical" rituals, which include initiation.

Initiation

Initiation is a psychological and spiritual regeneration. Initiation is the process of renewing commitments to the higher purpose and aspirations of life. In an initiatory process, life potential is enhanced. It includes larger spheres of influence into which the human individual can live and act. Initiation is an expansion of the capacity to direct one's life. Initiation connects to the realms of the beings of nature and the beings of the cosmos, through the frameworks of one's culture. Initiation is the growth of consciousness to integrate the will to be oneself at a given time and place. It can happen and does happen at any moment when, through their circumstances, human individuals are separated from what is familiar. We are turned toward the unknown. Characteristics of this turn are uncertainty and the search for meaning. We encounter various dilemmas as we navigate the initiatory path. We remake the agreements that connect us to our life's purpose. Finding coherence within the primary agreement of our life, we call the return coming home to self. We are able then to integrate this self into community. Where we can serve and where we are seen as the bearer of gifts, our creative inner expression is toward the world. All of the separation and dilemmas are then understood. They are necessary to the achieving of wholeness and integrity of spirit and right relationship to the world.

Initiation breaks through into the psyche. Initiation radically alters our way of being in daily life. Initiation awakens the dream carried within human souls from times beyond their current existence. These dreams are compelling and relevant to the Self each of us truly is. They are carriers of energies that build the capacities that exist in every human being to fulfill the purpose of our lives through our creative endeavors. These dreams inspire the conversations that become *indabas*—the telling of our life stories, of what could be true in our lives if we pursue the course of our destinies with intention and courage. Such dreams awaken the capacity to heal, to restore the vital balance and the energetic flows in the body for the recovery of their optimum function. These dreams are a source of life flow. They unite the discontinuities of perception to create memory, insight, and understanding of the experiences that have fallen into the unconscious. These dreams transform into a conscious awareness and the will to act. Such a dream in mythology is Isis restoring Osiris/Asar to life.

During initiation, the capacity for awareness is expanded. Our spirit of learning attends to the creation of new knowledge and an intuitive certainty that our life is purposeful, meaningful, and resourceful. Our language moves from being profane to being sacred. We give our word to each other as a gift, for the purpose of making covenants of the heart—agreeing on what it is we must decide for in order to fulfill our lives. We enter the world of prophecy, where what could become true is revealed because we seek this form of second sight, which enables us to see through our fears and alter our perceptions of each other. We behold the true nature of what stands in our midst, a larger presence that holds our life together and holds our worlds together. We can call this our future, and we can share it.

I do feel that every human being enters initiation every day, but because we usually are unaware of this and don't have the correct benchmarks to observe its progress, we don't attend to it consciously. If we were to examine our life circumstances, however, we would see a higher spiritual force is constantly interrupting them. This force organizes and directs our lives toward their higher potentials. As it is, we don't socialize our consciousness so that we know we are in initiation. We can, however, learn to observe this process. We can turn our daily observation into a ritual. We can create the rituals to help the mind stabilize itself long enough for the shift of consciousness to happen. We can do that at any moment through our own effort.

LOVE AND TRUTH

Through the power of love one can restore life—life being the connection that a person makes to the inherent self-sufficiency to always decide for the truth, because it's knowable.

Antonio and Robert

The community of Watts, where I have worked since the summer of 1987, is a community with deep roots of cultural struggle punctuated by episodes of social violence. Watts has served as a residence for many cultural groups, from the indigenous peoples of the Los Angeles area to Chinese immigrants, migrating blacks from the South, and the current historical presence of Chicano groups. The fires that erupted in Watts in 1965 during the civil disturbances of the Civil Rights era were put out on the surface, but in the core of the community there still burns a passionate flame for a new course of life and meaning.

At the height of its communal activism, in the 1960s, Watts bore the flag for an active Civil Rights Movement and pioneered a spirit of self-determination for communities of color, which sought their American liberties in light of their historic and emerging cultural self-knowledge. Watts served as a crossroads for the radical change that was happening in Los Angeles and radiating out to other cities along the West Coast. It served as the heart for the artistic, creative impulses flowing from the East Coast to the West. Watts in the city of Los Angeles was an economic and cultural corridor for what was emerging as a new social political movement in California.

The community of Watts is known to be central to the rise of the Bloods and Crips gangs in Los Angeles. They emerged as a result of the falling apart of progressive political movements and the loss of civil leadership in the late '60s and early '70s. In 1992, the fires erupted again in the city of Los Angeles, giving rise to new cultural struggles and a generation of young people seeking new methods of self-knowledge and economic security. The historical conditions that influenced the loss of economic opportunities created a vacuum that was filled by hopelessness, violence, and a drug-fueled economy.

The creation of gangs for the purposes of the drug economy became more intentional, through the placement of drugs into the cultural space both by organized criminal elements from outside and by those from within who utilized drugs to sustain their rival gang territories through mutual destruction.

During the early 1970s in Los Angeles, gangs took on a more organized form of recruiting membership for the purpose of violence toward each other. The more they were invested in the drug market, the more the sense of the historical struggle for civil rights was lost. The conflicts that now exist among the groups identified as gangs are perpetuated without any understanding of the historical reasons of why the groups were originally formed, the purpose they serve, and the impact they've made.

What transpired in American cities—in Watts in 1965 and in Detroit, Newark, and many others—can be understood as an uprising of the spirit of change that could find no other way to be integrated into the American economic and social life. The absence of agreements for what was possible for the lives of millions of blacks burned passionately in the flames that erupted in these American cities. When the investigation by the National Advisory Committee on Civil Disorder was completed in March of 1968, they found and reported that there had been no organized effort behind the uprisings and riots in these cities, but that social and political forces that had placed blacks in structured isolation called ghettos had fostered the conditions for this unrest. The commission reported that America was on a path of becoming two societies—one black, one white—separate and definitely unequal.

The recommendations from the Committee were for specific institutions to be created for the integration of blacks into American civil life. The Civil Rights Movement, however, struggled without government support for meeting the economic needs of millions of blacks. Blacks who—out of a consciousness initiated by their struggles—wanted to work freely for their self-sufficiency and for a shared society now found themselves exiled into a culture of despair. This provoked a spontaneous revolt against such structures as the ghetto, aimed at burning away the decay that had been built around them. This expression of the youth in American cities brought the nation's attention to what was awakened in them as the will to aspire and to participate in the shaping of the fundamental agreements of political and social life. It was a calling for true initiation.

In 1991, I was an academic advisor to a group of young students from King Drew Magnet High School of Medicine and Science in the Los Angeles unified school district. This school caters to students who are interested in medicine and science, as well as those who need various forms of social and academic assistance to meet their academic and career goals. One member of this group was a young man named Robert. He lived in the Nickerson Gardens Housing Project community and showed a strong interest in a life path beyond the boundaries now so deeply established by the lack of employment opportunities and the high concentration of gangs. We started to work on preparation for his graduation from high school and plans for college. For two years, our conversations were about plans for his future. At the end of this time, he succeeded in graduating and began to apply for entrance into college, with a view to a medical career.

In February of 1995, as my own path unfolded from the experience of my relationship with Lazar and his death, I chose to give attention to the inner striving of a number of students with whom I was now meeting, young men who wanted their lives to have meaning. Robert was one of these. During one of my visits with him, I invited him to a retreat that Mosaic was sponsoring as part of its mentorship initiative with young people. For the first time, we were inviting young people from different parts of the country, some of whom were involved with gangs and others who faced life circumstances that put them at a disadvantage or serious risk. Robert agreed to join the retreat.

One day shortly before the retreat was to begin, while I was waiting for Robert to return home, his cousin Antonio entered the house. He turned to me and asked, "Don't I know you?" I said we had seen each other before, but didn't really know each other. So we introduced ourselves again. When we shook hands, it felt as if I had taken more than his hands—as if we had exchanged some level of trust.

After he left, I asked Robert if he would invite Antonio to attend the retreat with us, and Robert replied, "I don't think he would go to something like this." I asked Robert to do it anyway and see what Antonio would say. Robert did ask him and, whatever the creative forces were behind this meeting, Antonio decided he would come. As it turned out, this would make a big difference in his life and in the lives of a number of people at this retreat; for he brought with him a task that—once we encountered it—we knew we would have to carry for a long time, walking him through a complex future.

The retreat was in Northern California, in the city of Fairfax, and there were 120 of us gathered there. Attending were about fifty-five young men; the others were older participants, mentors, and teachers for the retreat. This event proved to us how unprepared we were for the profound depth of what these young men carried: the stories of their lives, the wounds, the violence, the betrayals, the anger, and the search for help and healing.

The various teachers that were involved with this retreat—Michael Meade; Miguel Rivera, healer and holder of Native American tradition; Martin Prachtel, author and holder of Mayan initiation tradition; Jack Kornfield, author and Buddhist teacher; and several others—formulated out of their own experience, knowledge, and creativity new structures and activities to address the needs of the youth who were present.

Robert and Antonio made their way into the event with a great sense of enthusiasm, until as they and others shared their life stories, they began to experience in a new way their own inner struggles. I remember Robert's wanting to leave because he had lost two valuable things. When I inquired further as to why he was so upset, he told me that within the previous month four of his friends had been killed in gang violence. As he shared this, his grief over this loss and the weight of this way of living emerged. I understood that he was carrying it by himself—and it was too much. He then asked if I could help him. I said, "Yes, I will try." Robert decided he would stay for the rest of the event. He recovered not just one of his possessions, a ring that was valuable to him—more importantly, he also recovered a sense of his direction in life and a feeling that he was not alone in the world.

Antonio shared his story with the entire group of youth and men who were there. It was a sharing of profound pain and loss. He hadn't believed it was possible to find anyone, particularly in a group of strangers, who could understand or care for what he carried. It was the most intense five days we'd ever had in hosting this retreat over the last four or five years. It was Mosaic's first youth event and it opened up for us a new practice of learning of how to work with gangs, their violence, their loss, and the disillusionment of our youth in a culture that's forgotten how to care for them.

One of the things that especially anchored the young men who were present with us and allowed them to experience the deep imagination of their own lives was the activity of making masks. Each person was paired with another and would take a turn in making a mask by placing plaster on the face of his partner. The masks were expressions of their own sense of self. When this process was over, they were all asked to paint their masks in preparation for a ritual that would be conducted at a later stage of the retreat. I remember Antonio's mask, in particular, because in making it he had drawn from his memory some deeper memory from beyond his immediate cultural exposure. The motif of the memory was what he painted into his mask. It was red and black, with all the cosmograms associated with initiation. I remember how moved everyone was upon seeing this design. This was a creative process that would inspire Antonio and shape the memory that he would recall to support himself in the difficult days that lay ahead.

We returned to Los Angeles around the 19th of February, when I learned immediately that there was a warrant out for Antonio 's arrest. His photograph and name were mentioned on the local news in connection with an alleged gang incident in which he was accused of being involved. We, the community of men that hosted this conference, had before us now an immense crisis in the life of someone with whom we had made a commitment, someone we now cared for.

Our intention to give support to Antonio took the form of helping him see his future and be able to live it out. He spent the next five years in a series of trials before he was finally convicted in the fifth of these. He was given a sentence of forty-four years to life in jail, which was appealed and overturned. In an effort to avoid a sixth trial, his lawyer asked for the help of the Mosaic community—which had now spent more than five years with Antonio in this process—to support a petition for a plea bargain. Several of us were invited to meet with the prosecutors, and after this meeting, Antonio's lawyer was able to agree, on his behalf, to a sentence of twelve years, six of which he had already served. This was still hard for Antonio to accept, but we supported him in thinking through all the alternatives and the risks of being again on trial. He did accept it and completed this sentence within the California State Prison System, returning home in April of 2007. In the framework of our work in Shade Tree and Mosaic, we call this process "walking with." The core of our mentorship of Antonio occurred while he was in prison—between the ages of nineteen and thirty-one—through letters, telephone calls, and visits.

Antonio's initiation and rites of passage from youth to adulthood took place in one of the hardest prison systems in our nation. He had to rely on the glimpses of stories and myths, the conversations and friendships he had formed in his five days at the retreat with us. He held on to many of the images of that week—the trees, the quietness of the night, the stars, the songs and poems, the drums. He recalled these images and retold these words to himself on many hard nights and days in the aloneness of a cell far away from family and friends and his child. As part of a dedication to him and others who were in prison during our retreats, we would place a table of remembrance for each of them in the midst of our meals. And this is still done for those who are in prison. For Antonio we did it for six years, and to him—and others like him who have returned home—we can say, "Welcome back."

During the time of Antonio's incarceration, I continued my work with Robert to pursue the goals that he had before him. He had applied to the University of California, Los Angeles to pursue a degree as an X-ray technician. As part of the application process, we engaged in all the preparation necessary, which included interviewing and completing an essay about his future. I remember the day he received his acceptance letter and the powerful impression it made on him and his family that he had more to look forward to in his life. After a couple of weeks, though, another letter arrived, telling him his acceptance had been revoked. The letter said it had been a mistake and that he should reapply the following year. This rejection went all the way to his heart. It cast a shadow over his vision of his future and extinguished his trust that there could be a way out of his despair. To have worked so hard and to have been accepted and then rejected was for him a final blow to his hope of having a career.

He struggled with this for the next year, even though he pursued community college courses. Fate tempted him through his need to earn a living. What was present and compelling all around him was a world in which drug dealing was the income of choice for a great many of the youth that had no way out, no bridge, no help to find another way of life. Fate took his hand and he allowed himself to be led into this underworld, where money and the lure of its influence prevailed and his higher goals retreated. This eventually led to his being arrested and convicted of a conspiracy to distribute drugs, and he was sentenced to six-and-a-half years in federal prison.

This is where we engaged in our deepest work, again through letters, telephone calls, and visits. In prison, Robert became very proficient in exploring the ideas behind the economic possibilities for work. He studied and read and cultivated a tremendous interest in the question: What is destiny? His questions led to some remarkable mentorship conversations about the process of being in prison. He and I entered a deep dialogue about what is prison and what is it to be exiled and how do you transform that? Although Robert was physically in prison, it felt as if we were always in dialogue: that we had access to worlds of possibilities and could enter agreements that could make those possibilities attainable. The community of Shade Tree and Mosaic provided a continued source of inspiration and help to him, as to Antonio and others in similar circumstances. Robert returned home in September of 2006. He has since served as a mentor to many other young people in his community and with other intervention agencies in Los Angeles.

We look for the tree in a time and place when it fulfills a need to protect us from the elements in the larger environment. It is a natural sanctuary when the conditions are conflicting and the time is uncertain and the territory dangerous.

8
SHADE TREE

The Story of the Tree from the Yoruba

According to the Yoruba people of the West Coast of Africa, a very long time ago before there was anything but sky and water, the Creator, Olorun, lowered a great chain from the sky to the waters below. Oduduwa, Olorun's son, climbed down this chain from the sky to the waters. He brought with him a handful of dirt, and when he reached the waters he threw the dirt upon them. Oduduwa also brought with him a chicken that he had tucked under his arm, and this chicken had five toes. Oduduwa placed the chicken upon the dirt, and as all chickens will do, it began to scratch and scatter the dirt. With its five toes it was able to scratch and scratch the dirt, until the whole dry Earth was formed. In the center of this new world, Oduduwa planted a palm nut, and from this nut a magnificent tree grew with sixteen branches.

The Story of the Tree from the Bushmen

The Bushmen of central Africa say that once a long time ago the people and animals lived beneath the earth with Kaang, the Creator of All Life. Here underneath the earth, people and animals lived together peacefully. They could speak one another's language. There was always plenty of food, and it was always light even though there was no sunlight. Kaang decided that he would go to the earth above and make a beautiful world there as well.

First he created a great tree, with branches that stretched over the entire world. Then he began to shape the world around the tree, with rivers and mountains and lakes and the bush. At the base of the tree, he dug a hole that reached all the way down into the world below, where all the people and animals lived, and he led the first man up the hole.

The man sat down on the edge of the hole, and soon the first woman also came up out of it. Eventually all the people were gathered at the foot of the tree, looking around them at the beauty of the world they had just entered. They were in awe. Next, Kaang helped the animals climb out of the hole. Some of the animals came out of the hole so fast that they just kept going from the roots of the tree all the way up into its branches.

Finally, all the animals and all the people were gathered under the branches of the great tree. Kaang then gave them his instructions. They were to live together peacefully and they were not to build any fires, he said, or evil would befall them. The people and the animals all gave their word. They saw no need to build fires, as they had never needed them in the world below. Kaang the Creator left the people and animals under the great tree.

And then something happened that had never happened in the world below. The sun began to sink beneath the horizon and darkness began to fall. The people and all the animals watched this great change, and when the sun disappeared, the people began to feel cold because they had no fur as the animals had. They became afraid because they could no longer see as the animals could. They did not know what to do, and then at last a man said, "Let us build a fire. It will keep us warm, and we'll be able to see." Because they were afraid and cold, they forgot what the Creator had told them, and they built a fire.

When the animals saw the fire they became frightened and ran away from the people to the caves and the mountains. So now animals and people can no longer speak to one another, except sometimes when they happen upon each other under the great Shade Tree.

Earth as School of Love

The Earth is the school of love. Earth is where we form relationships and learn to connect through service for the sake of the whole. Nowhere else is this possible but on Earth. In this sense, Earth is the great evolutionary experiment, upon which the whole universe depends.

Earth and humanity are one, as humanity is one. There is no such thing as a single human being. A human being is always in relation. That is why Shade Tree exists—for our unfolding humanity. Becoming aware of Shade Tree and learning its ways allow us to become more fully human.

Shade Tree

Shade Tree is the gift of the capacity to change or be changed. Given to us by the gods, it is their—and our—best chance to fulfill the promise of the Earth, to cultivate the capacity to regenerate. Shade Tree is therefore our link with greater nature—the evolving future of earthly reality.

Shade Tree is a place or state of unconditional hospitality, welcome, and community. It stands tall. Its presence is deep-rooted in the earth. Its leafy boughs spread toward the horizons, arching as far as the eye can see into the heavens. Beneath it, in its shade, beings gather. Shade Tree provides a safe place, where people can always come together and strangers are always at home.

It is a home away from home, the heart of the village. Here we are most human and vulnerable. It is where we begin and end our journey and where we rest on the way between leaving and returning. You will always find friends sitting or standing beneath the tree, sheltered from the harshness of the elements, talking, laughing, telling stories, or just silently communing.

Sometimes, the more enterprising climb onto its branches to see who is coming. Or perhaps they want to see for themselves what lies beyond the horizon. Messages are left there. Shade Tree is a place of communication, of questions. Above all, Shade Tree is a crossroads. It is where Heaven and Earth, inner and outer, same and other—friend and foreigner—meet. Arriving, strangers will go straight to the Shade Tree to discover where they have come from and where they should go.

The origin of Shade Tree is unknown. It is said that no one planted it. As far as anyone knows, it has been there forever. The story is that it is as old as the universe. It is said that its roots are above, in heaven. Some say its seed was sown in the beginning time. African elders call it the cosmic tree. They say it stands at the heart of the world. According to their teachings, its branches reach to the four comers, the four directions, and its vertical axis connects Heaven and Earth, above and below, past, present, and future.

The tree is symbolic of the vertical axis that establishes the spiritual center in a person and between two people. It is what allows us to have a shared sense of reality and an inner understanding of self. That shared understanding enables us to create the world of probability by deciding through our agreements on very specific things. This vertical axis allows us to follow a path in the earth to cultivate love for who we are becoming.

Those who know the tree intimately know that this is true, because for them the tree bears its fruits in the seasons of their lives. New growth is always flourishing on this tree. It is always putting out leaves and tiny, hardly perceptible blossoms. If the branches and leaves are broken through the hardships of life, the sap from the beginning time cannot reach the branches, and they wither and drop off. This is a sign of difficult times.

Myths and legends throughout the world speak of Shade Tree as the tree of love and knowledge. Many stories tell of the capacities—new ways of knowing—that the Tree can bestow. The elders say that these capacities are the seeds of the future, which will create the new forms that evolution requires of us. It is also called the tree of imagination and memory, for it is the true source of the deep loving, which is true knowledge. The elders say that, for a human being to know, he or she must be connected to Shade Tree. For this reason, in the old tales, its branches are always filled with birds, messengers of the gods, who bring dreams and visions of what is not yet, but still to come. Human beings and gods alike look to Shade Tree for guidance, meaning, and medicine.

Shade Tree is also the tree of the ancestors, and of the ancestors of the ancestors—going back to the first ancestor of all. It is the perpetual source for the continuity of inspiration. Everyone recognizes Shade Tree's generosity and its profound power to regenerate. Universally accessible, the elders call it the Tree of Life.

Being connected to the tree leads to change and growth. Being at the tree allows us to receive help and to be oriented to changes happening within. It helps us to receive aid and to be oriented toward changes taking place within. It helps us remember where to be and when, and it helps us find the road back to authenticity, the meaning of life, and the place of belonging.

Shade Tree Foundation

Shade Tree Multi-cultural Foundation is a community of mentors that began meeting in 1995 and became a nonprofit organization in 2000. We have come together over the last twenty years to share in *indaba* the life stories of those we have met and worked with. We hold regular *indabas* to support this mentorship initiative. Shade Tree is a pathway of knowledge that has been created from the destiny paths of a diverse group of people. Our mentors are working within a variety of professions and other social organizations, but the common thread is the ongoing *indaba* that we hold to support our own practice and mentoring work.

Shade Tree offers trainings that empower mentors to work in difficult and demanding situations including schools, community groups, human development organizations, and prisons. It is a multicultural organization, dedicated to the cultural specificity of each person's path as well as supporting the capacity for cross-cultural relationships.

The founding of Shade Tree came out of a spontaneous recognition of a need to provide mentorship and community for the youth we invited to the Mosaic retreat back in 1995. It was also inspired by the work I did with Lazar and the openness I felt toward Robert and Antonio and many others in the community of Los Angeles where I live and work. Shade Tree's primary work of mentoring was never intended to become a standard program. Our inspiration to mentor emerged out of the environment that put human lives at risk, the social context that challenges our creativity, and out of the resiliency of the inner life of an individual in search of meaning. More personally, it grew out of my own awakening to the reality that people each carry within themselves a unique memory that provides a paradigm of life, a specific way of being, distinct and free from the patterns of others.

Several others joined in the conversations to provide regular opportunity to involve these young people in this mentoring work and to formulate together an understanding of the rites of passage from isolation into community. Among those who committed time at the beginning of Shade Tree's mentoring process were Vance Aniebo, Jordan Good, Miguel Rivera, Tim Smith, Shelly Tuchluk, Pasqual Torres, Robert Akil Bell, and many others. We worked as an open community for five years, making ourselves available out of our own interest and sense of calling. We met weekly for *indabas* around our own development and our involvement in the lives of many young people. In doing this, we all discovered something unique about our lives that inspires what we share with the youth we mentor. It has come to be understood that mentors serve out of the dreams they are living, out of the mistakes they've made, and out of their own capacities to give and receive. They create the specific context for each relationship they cultivate and decide on the boundaries that limit time and availability of whatever resources they choose to dedicate to this work.

Each person who is mentored creates a specific framework for what is needed in our work. They choose their mentor based on qualities that best support the inner sense of freedom they are striving to attain. We call it "genius to genius" mentoring; the youth sees in the mentor the specific quality that allows their own genius to be remembered. This means that a mentor cannot be simply assigned by the organization, as is typically done. What determines the connection is the specific nature of what the youth is striving to see and the unpredictable flash of spirit that illuminates the heart and mind of the youth seeking initiation, radical change, or a relationship for *indaba*. Central to our initial work was conversation, ritual and healing, engagement in the arts, and capacity building for work and civil participation. All this continues to be essential, now that Shade Tree is a foundation.

Shade Tree was formed as a response to a critical need in the life of our society, the breakdown of community, and the absence of normative spaces for youth development. The lives of young people are placed at risk when they feel abandoned and exiled from any sense of relationship and purpose in life. We call this a crossroads, a social situation in which the direction of life leads to the edge, to either self-inflicted violence or conflict with others and deeper social violence.

As mentors, we take the initiative to encounter young people who are seeking a relationship, offering a possibility of change. We begin by making ourselves available to our youth, knowing that the cultural times and spaces in which they live are fragile and uncertain. We strive to recognize when young people are seeking mentorship through the questions they ask or, at times, when it is obvious that without someone reaching out to them, they will most likely lose their way. The cultivated awareness of mentors enables them to know how to sense the presence of a young person in trouble and offer help. Often their capacity to remember their own difficult journeys in life makes it possible for this encounter to be real and meaningful, so that the young person feels secure enough to come to a place of sanctuary and support. This mentoring, then, can take place under the sacred power of the Shade Tree, guided by the presence of the destiny forces that bring people together.

Reflections on Mentoring

In our society, mentorship is generally looked at as a big-brother/big-sister type of support, but as we understand it in Shade Tree, it goes much deeper. It relates directly to the human quest for meaning, the longing to connect to the deeper truth of initiation: psychological and spiritual regeneration of the capacity for right relationship to one's true purpose in life. From this perspective, morality is not just a question of the action based on traditional concepts of right and wrong. Morality or moral memory is a cognitive awareness of the true self. If I am able to transcend all the social conflicts and given circumstances of my life by awakening to the faculty that gives it meaning, I will discover my will to act consistent with my higher purpose.

For example, resolving a gang conflict often begins by finding where in life the person being mentored has experienced betrayal. An enemy becomes an enemy because of a repeated betrayal. A person can be helped to overcome the sense of loss and mistrust that the experience of betrayal has generated. This can be done only by helping a person recover the intention of trust, by helping a person to participate in creating an agreement through letting go of the expectation that someone is going to hurt him. He can then strengthen his own capacity to heal the wounds—the wounds that were predisposing him to engage in violence. In this, mentorship supports the capacity to give meaning to his life. Mentorship supports working through the various conflicts and reaching new levels of agreement.

Mentorship begins as a relationship between two people who have found each other at a time in life when one is seeking to be seen. It is a shared journey into the memory of what has been lived and what is to be lived. It is a conversation about past and future, a conversation across time and into the deep recesses of the self. It is an archetypal relational space that transmits the love of wisdom for a unique dialogue between two people who have found one thing in common—love for who they are and love of the life they see in each other. It is a way of seeing and being seen, a recalling of what has given shape to character and destiny. Mentors are those who have journeyed longer and survived the twists and turns in life's roads and have been able to recover from their mistakes; who have known the wounds and betrayals, the hardships and controversies that challenge and enable us to learn and live into who we are. Mentorship is the telling of stories that continue to be created by those who tell them. It is also the listening into the stories by those who long to know the mysteries that are revealed through life's quest.

Validating "Who I Am"

How do we recognize the mentor? If we examine our own lives, particularly during adolescence, we recognize that we are looking for a particular quality in another human being that can allow us to authenticate and to validate "who I am." In order to play this role, the qualities most needed by the mentor are nonjudgmental attentiveness and a capacity to understand. These two strengths are what the youth inwardly assesses in seeking out someone who can provide this form of support. This assessment is the first step in the search for a mentor.

Young people are looking to step out of the isolation that adolescence brings them into. This isolation occurs because at a certain time human beings become aware of a deeper place within themselves that is unknown. Each of us carries within ourselves—past, present, and future—a seed from the Tree of Life. In adolescence, the psychic forces awaken in us recognition that the past in oneself holds the ancestral memory. The future holds purpose, and the present sustains the dynamic tension of how I choose to be. During this time we require a witness, another human being who can understand this mystery and stand in total acceptance of "who I am," as that begins to emerge. We can't step into that by ourselves. This is *sawubona.*

So this witnessing begins the initiation of the human being at a time when we know that in order to live we must be understood. If the isolation remains for too long, the youth experiences a type of fear in the consciousness that leads to doubt of the inner forces that are guiding destiny. The inner forces that are enhanced by reflection, contemplation, and aspiration support the youth's action toward purpose and the inner feeling of security and trust. What strengthens the youth's resolve for continued striving is the attentiveness of others. Attentiveness is central in a mentoring relationship. The absence of attentiveness by adults in the life of a youth leads to a loss of these inner free forces: the capacity to question, to wonder, and to imagine the "what if" potential of the soul.

Without a relationship of this nature, inner conflict arises within the youth. This leads to self-doubt, a turning inward of thoughts. This leads eventually to self-destructive acts and violence. In the absence of parents, mentors, and elders—relationships that stand as agreements for normative development—the youth experiences a state of isolation, and the inner conflict becomes external violence over time. There is a total lack of interest in any agreement with another human being. Increasingly there is a loss of interest in meaning, love, and eventually, even self. This can result in a radical lack of self-awareness; the basic experience is simply one of existence. There is no striving, no truth—or at most, a diminished sense of both.

The Genesis Pathway

The Genesis Pathway is the beginning of a relationship that supports the discovery of how young people can find their way in the world. It is an inquiry into the inner space of self-awareness and self-development. It is the cultivation of capacities to negotiate the social world in which they must live. It is a co-creation of a conversation that enables them to express their own voices. It is to discover the inherent values of their spirit. It is to trust the guide who brings them to new thresholds of change.

A first step in such an approach to mentorship is to recognize that a specific type of conversation is being asked for. The mentor recognizes that the youth is asking for a relational space for the purpose of investigating his particular life circumstances. This request expresses a specific self-interest that reminds the mentor of something in his own life. Once awakened in the mentor, this memory generates increased attention to the specific nature of what wants to be attended to in the youth.

It begins with what the mentor remembers as the "edge," a place where he, himself, stood looking into the world of the unknown. Mentorship occurs best when this place is reestablished. Not as an exact knowing of what to do in a particular circumstance, but as a capacity for improvisation. Mentorship is based on the cultivated wisdom of what the mentor had decided for previously in his own life and what experience has since strengthened and verified as meaningful and true. This exchange supports the youth in deciding what choices could work for him, not in a prescriptive way, but by way of trust and a clarifying of options.

The intention of mentoring is to prepare young people to be alone and, when alone, to be able to decide how to overcome tendencies of fear and doubt. Mentoring is the building of this capacity to access choices and to stand responsibly within those choices. It is not that mistakes will not happen. There are now capacities to help them understand how to remain feeling certain about who they are as individuals.

The mentor attends to the capacity in the young to be attentive to what's given in their life and what must change in their own application of will. They learn how they must now engage in making their life practical through attention to the details and everyday demands that show up in their lives. The mentor teaches them how to create a context for remembering the important steps in thinking through what they feel. The mentor gives a way to think through what they experience in the environment around them.

True mentorship becomes a conversation, created out of the young person's lived experiences, an ongoing *indaba*. The self-knowledge generated through this dialogue supports new degrees of understanding. It prepares them to turn toward a deeper memory, which we can call the wisdom of the soul or the ancestral memory. This, in turn, prepares them for conscious initiation and an ability to face the outer uncertainties of life with increasing inner certainty. We co-create the world as we walk into it initiating our will, strengthening our perception, and choosing our conversations and relationships. These are the processes of being in community.

Every such experience cultivated through mentorship leads the young person into a sense of belonging, belonging to their own path of life, secure in their will to give meaning to reality. It prepares them to enter into relationship with community. They can draw on the capacities of others to develop their gifts further and can receive from others the support and encouragement to keep living.

Those who are mentored in this way often become mentors to others out of a sense of gratitude for having been witnessed at a time when their lives required genuine contact with another person. This experience remains active in them, and a sense of responsibility toward anyone seeking mentorship is awakened in them. What is planted as a seed in the life of a youth later blossoms into a capacity to give and serve. The sacred tree that stands within the center of the human being, rooted in ancestral wisdom and branching out toward the worlds of possibilities, serves as a place of sanctuary for anyone finding himself on the crossroads of life, where the wanderer can stop and find a moment to ask, "Who am I, where am I?" and have someone present to respond.

Shade Tree's mentoring work in Los Angeles is about finding the way to Self. That is, initiating one's path out of the isolation and violence inherited through years of generational misfortune and willful persecution. Self-knowledge is the redemptive act for fulfilling the prophecy of bringing history current and deciding how to dedicate deeper service to it. Our communal work through Shade Tree embraces multi-cultural practices for the explicit purpose of supporting human beings to cross the various boundaries of the soul that are defined by cultural inheritances and ancestral legacies different to each group and different in each generation. This work of finding the source from which these cultural paradigms emerge is the primary objective of working on a pedagogy for freedom, a process of self-knowing.

Central, then, to all the mentoring work of Shade Tree is our commitment to initiation. Initiation is intended to serve practical life, to serve day-to-day needs. In the examination of the history of our work and the people who have created it, we know that each of us has found something in ourselves that we are now able to share with others. We can define the stages of our development and the capacities that brought us to our own understanding of the stages of initiation: when we entered it, how long we've been in the deep dilemma it entails, and the possibilities for emergence into a shared awareness of a greater future. In this work we endeavor to develop in others the love for cultivating the world as a genuine place where we share what nature and spirit give us.

9
ANCESTRAL MEMORY

Shrine

A shrine is an icon of prayer, a portal to the other world. Here messages are sent and received and medicines prepared.

The shrine is the heart and hearth of our sanctuary. It is dedicated to the sacred. Sustained by love, it is a place where gifts are offered and vows—commitments—are made. It is a continuous reminder of the nature of our task—to find a shared meaning for life.

Metaphysically, the shrine enacts our relationship to the supernatural world. It betokens a ritual approach to life. Through it, we formalize our observance of the sacred and make our experience sacred. By sacred, I mean what demands sacrifice from us. To make something sacred, we must search our inner parts for what we must give to witness wholeness or healing. We are reminded of wholeness—our own and the wholeness of all—by being conscious, present, and attentive at the shrine.

A moment at the shrine is a moment of surrender. A "descent" occurs. There is a break in time and, in this gap, deeds can be vowed, decisions made. In these moments, we can carry something for the whole Earth. We can create "new" time that can flow into the Earth. We can become human time-spirits and incarnate something new for the sake of the Earth's unfolding. The shrine then becomes an Imagination we can hold before us as a guide for the future. It is a way of contacting a larger aspect of living than our own self-involved life. In this sense, it is recognition of our essential "servant" nature—that we are made to serve, for service.

The shrine can be observed through the qualities of the elements that define the ecology of the natural world—earth, fire, water, mineral, and nature. This whole ecology is a shrine in and of itself that constitutes the elements that serve human life processes. Through the understanding of these elements we can experience our inner cosmology and the deeper meaning of our life is understood. Approaching the shrine in this way we approach a place—or state—where spirit and earth, nature and culture meet. We call this the pool of ancestral memory. Standing on its banks, emptied of self, we can call on the ancestors for help.

CREDO MUTWA

Early spring in 1998, a friend invited me to a gathering. He wanted me to meet a Zairian by the name of Kikosa. He didn't explain what the gathering was about. When I arrived, after being introduced to the hosts, I met Kikosa. He explained that he had just returned from South Africa, where he had lived and worked with Credo Mutwa, the Zulu Sanusi. He said that Credo Mutwa had sent a message to us in the United States, and he wanted to play the tape to the gathering. The tape was called "The Shining Path," referring to the old goddess religion in South Africa. It was also the outline of the training that is done for the healers—the *Ingayas* (the Warriors of the Moon) and the *Sangoma* (Healers of the Drum). On this tape Credo Mutwa talked about the Shining Path, the beginning of African spirituality, which he knew was to become active again in the emerging age. His voice was melodic, the embodiment of *indaba*.

Implicit in what he said was a prophetic teaching of the return of two gods who had helped humanity in the past, when the last world was changing, and would return to do the same again as humanity and the world changed again. Credo Mutwa's outline of the training of the *Ingaya* was like reliving my childhood. These were all things I did on my own to develop my discipline of mind and body to respect the spiritual world. Immediately I felt a connection to his voice and teachings. I recognized a call, an invitation.

At the close of the evening, I spoke to Kikosa. I told him I was very interested in this area of study and research. I also told him of my work with Malidoma and found out that he, too, had worked with Malidoma. He told me that he was returning to continue his work with Credo Mutwa and insisted that I should visit Credo Mutwa. I agreed that I would consider doing so.

As Kikosa shared with me of what he knew of Credo Mutwa's work and purpose in the world and the reason for him sending this message to us in the United States, I reflected on a previous incident that I had experienced. Several months earlier, I had attended a friend's wedding-anniversary party in Los Angeles. I arrived at Glenda's home, greeted her, her husband, and other friends. Sometime during the evening I went to the living room to take a seat. There was one seat available next to a white gentleman sitting quietly reflecting to himself. I thought for a moment whether or not I should interrupt by taking the seat next to him. I decided that I would. Before we could introduce ourselves, he asked, "When are you going to South Africa?" There was no context for his question and I was surprised by what he asked. I replied, "I have no intention of going to South Africa." He said, "You don't know it now, but you will. And you won't know your work until you go." I said, "How do you know this?" He said, "I'm a psychic." I laughed, thinking, isn't everyone?

A few months later, I flew to South Africa and was to be there for five days. Credo Mutwa was expecting me. Kikosa had made the arrangements and I went straight to Credo Mutwa's home in Johannesburg. Meeting him was beyond my expectations. Credo Mutwa sees so deeply into the human being—he saw so deeply into me—that he knew much better than I did, what I was there for. We would sit in *indaba* from morning to evening, only interrupted by meals, breaks, and siestas. During these sessions, I was taken directly into the ancestral world by his stories. His capacity to paint pictures of healing through his words was truly remarkable. His reverence for the ancestors, which he called by name, and the spirits with whom he shared a deep relationship, affected the space within which we talked.

Credo Mutwa provided me with the rituals to bring balance to my life path. He provided the spiritual framework for understanding how to receive and utilize the ancestral guidance and medicine. It put together contexts of my life that I'm still able to draw from after those few days of *indaba*. Credo Mutwa or Baba is the last *Sanusi* in the Zulu tradition, the highest initiate in that cultural tradition, the keeper of the relics of the ancient priests. A *Sanusi* is one who embodies the total memory of the tribal imagination and who can travel the time corridors of the soul life, the collective consciousness of the people, one who is responsible for maintaining the archive of ancestral wisdom.

As we were talking serendipitously, with no forethought or planning. I told him the story of the personal myth I had written and asked him if he had ever heard of the Seventh Shrine. Baba laughed, and said with evident pleasure, "But you have written the story of your own birth!"

I asked him to tell me more. He said, "Yes. It is the Shrine of *Imani,* which is the Swahili word for 'Faith.'" This term was familiar to me as the seventh principle of the *Engosu Saba*, one of the principles of *Kwanzaa.* Baba said, "It is the shrine that is coming to be. There is no teaching for it. You will have to do it out of your own intention. In fact, you are already doing it." He added that I would not find any teachers to guide me, because I already knew what it was about and would encounter it every time I asked for it.

And so a new turn of my life began. I discovered that stories of the Seven Shrines existed in African lore as a way of speaking about the cycles of the evolution of consciousness. Credo Mutwa explored with me the stories of the prophecies held by the elders of the Zulu people and other peoples in Africa. He told of the great elders that were part of holding the gateways open for certain possibilities of world events that involve Africans and Europeans in South Africa and other parts of the world. He spoke of the Middle Passage and the mystery teachings about the journeys over the great waters. He spoke about the guidance that I would receive as someone who was brought to him by the ancestors to be given specific help to be part of the work in relationship to these prophecies. He felt that many of us in America would play a role in the unfolding of the making of these covenants for the world.

The evening of the second day with him culminated in a ritual during which he placed a necklace around my neck. He didn't say much about it. He just said it belonged to a sacred elder. I later learned that it was used to access the Seventh Shrine. He presented a second one, which was made while I was there by a *Sangoma*, or medicine woman. The second contained, conferred by a signature, a name that would be my initiation name, by which I would call into being my relationship with the spiritual world.

I chose at this point to use the term Baba, a word of respect, to refer to this great teacher because of my personal experience of feeling the connection with the power of his heart, for the truth that he has seen, and lived in relationship to the continuity of the deep wisdom of African thought. His life embodies a sacrifice that has cost him to be exiled from the larger community of elders. It has cost him the loss of life within his family and several attempts on his own life for this disclosure of the knowledge that he held. This disclosure was his attempt to honor the prophecies into which he was initiated. The disclosure of this sacred knowledge was absolutely necessary for the making of the deeper agreements between cultures, the preservation of the knowledge of the sacred medicines within the natural world, the reformulation of the initiation methods for the development of the people they serve and the sharing of the great epic stories for the waking of the mind to the mysteries.

As a *Sanusi*, Baba tells the stories that give rise to the deep traditions held in South Africa and to the cosmologies held in other parts of the world. He is able to relate the missing elements of the historical worldviews in order to provide a continuity of relationship for supporting a shared future. Baba is a singer of songs of the stars. He provides a context of study and practice, ritual and divination of things hidden in nature, the earth, and the elements that provide for us a renewed sense of the mystery schools that once flourished in African wisdom traditions. The relics that he invited me to see spanned hundreds of years of sacred ritual experiences, and were used for the governance of tribal and societal life, and are the source of deep medicine for the healing of people and place.

Our *indabas* started with the words, "Ask me any question you would like. May the ancestors speak to you." It was as if I was speaking to time itself with a humility beyond anything I had experienced in full service to my own lack of knowing, my devotion to understand, and my love for who I was now, knowing myself to be as result of his generous presence. The ancestors were with us in every *indaba*. When Baba laughed he inspired great joy in the heart, and when he cried it was the rivers of grief for he knew with his heart the commitments the spiritual world holds for us.

At the same time he witnesses what is being lost daily on the African continent through the natural resources of animal and human life, plant medicine and mineral wealth, relationships of people to people, village to village, nation to nation, and humanity to the spiritual world. He stands as a great tree on a vast plain of wilderness singing a song for the world to heal, pouring medicine into the vast rivers that run in our cultural veins, sounding the drum that new warriors of the Earth may find their place in defense of the nobility of the human spirit, the protection of the natural ecology of the world, and the preservation of our ancestral gifts.

The Dagara Cosmology

The cosmologies that I became interested in that were held in the African communities of memory included the cosmology of the Dagara people in Burkina Faso, West Africa. Through the study with Malidoma on the Dagara cosmology, the five elements and the shrines were introduced to me. The elements of earth, water, fire, mineral, and nature constitute the framework that informs the cosmology that the Dagara people use for initiation and cultural life. This cosmology teaches that the collective human group is comprised of individuals that represent each of the five elements. So a person's time of birth in a given year defines their elemental power or medicine, a predominant quality within their soul–spiritual nature that supports the ecology of consciousness of the group.

An individual is seen through this elemental presence in the world, and their initiation helps to bring this particular quality into full expression. The elements also determine the shrines and what they serve. There are initiation groups and elders around each elemental shrine and there are specific rituals to maintain, activate, and utilize them. Each shrine produces medicine specific to the element it represents. Within the Dagara cosmology I am considered a water person meaning that the element of water is what I brought into this world at birth in the year in which I was born. A significant part of my ritual training with this element, its medicine, the shrines, and my own life path occurred during my study in the Dagara cosmology. In extended conversation with Baba Credo Mutwa we focused on other qualities of the elements and the shrines that are carried within various other cosmologies in Africa.

In addition to the elemental shrines Baba spoke of the ancestral shrines, those that are passed on within the lineage of families and those that are passed on through initiations linking specific individuals to spiritual streams within the larger human spiritual context. In addition to this ancestral shrine the seventh shrine represents a specific initiation pathway, one that Baba described occurred in the spiritual significance of my birth. The Zulu astrology describes other portals of birth initiations beyond the Western astrological frameworks.

The Shrines

First Shrine: Earth

The first shrine is the Shrine of Earth. Its sign is Beginning or Primal Union. Earth, I understood from my African teachers, is the primal substance, the mothering force of the divine in the cosmos, into which humanity—every human being—incarnates, for every human being replicates in his or her development the evolution of the species. In this substance, the seed of consciousness is called to find the light of intention, of beginning, and growth.

For early humanity, the Earth shrine was the phase of collective, nomadic consciousness—a consciousness of quest and journey. The search was for soul, for what we might call psychic awareness of the waters of life. The call came from the future, the not-yet. Evolutionarily, it was a time when humanity was continuously, wordlessly, immersed in and led by dreams and visionary encounters with earthly and cosmic beings, that mediated the divine in all its forms. Consciousness was a form of silent recognition or witnessing. Death did not yet fully exist because it was only a threshold. The dead were as present as the living. Time was vertical. Human beings lived in the present, always toward the future.

Second Shrine: Water

The second shrine is the Shrine of Water, or the Soul. Its sign is *Intimacy.* In the progression of human evolution, with the Shrine of Water, humanity discovered soul and interior and exterior space as the capacity to reflect and imagine. What before was an outer dream was now experienced inwardly. The formative force of the world became active in human consciousness, taking hold of the will and instinctively forming the direction and course of destiny. Communication was spontaneous and telepathic, always free of judgment and resistance. Meaning was fluid, in perpetual becoming. Feeling was awakening. The sense of relatedness instinctively oriented shared goals.

Third Shrine: Fire

The third shrine is the Shrine of Fire. Its sign is *Intention.* With Fire, the psychic force became more concentrated in human consciousness in the ongoing human story. The light of intention began to penetrate the psyche. The decision to act—and the capacity to act freely—was now available to human beings and became part of human experience. Human beings began to experience the world, not as finished but as a process into which they could participate in co-creation of the world space. It was the foundation of culture. Through intention, human beings could add light to their own existence and to the shared possibilities for the continued growth of the Earth.

The element of Fire enhanced the quality of dream through an act of will that allowed humanity to bring creation into the worlds of probability. We were able to add to it through the activity of what was still wordless thinking. The formative power latent in the Shrine of Earth, or Beginning was now becoming active through the element of Fire. It is the capacity of the awakened ancestor, the original human seed.

Fourth Shrine: Mineral

The fourth shrine is the Mineral Shrine. Its sign is *Language*. We can see that with this shrine, the capacity for speech and the cultivation of language arose, allowing for the refinement of the promise of the Earth. At the same time, with language, arose a further concentration of the psyche into what is now called memory. As the power of memory crystallized and grew, death began to enter consciousness. The veil was half drawn and in this space a new sense of mind dawned that would become the medium for the embodiment of grace—food from heaven.

At the same time, through the same space, human beings began to cultivate the relationship between the starry heavens and the Earth. But this was not all. The mineral state of consciousness—the new mental sphere—allowed for the experience of dialogue and the exploration of the inner and outer principles of life. The possibility of science, philosophy, religion, and culture was born. In the story of human consciousness this was a time of great growth and risk. The "other" came into being. Separation began its rule. The forms individuated. Psyche took on personality and ego. The subconscious began and, with it, the possibility of subconscious formations, neuroses, and pathologies. Lies, too, became possible- and territoriality. Strife, unknown before, showed its fangs. Moral memory, the primal intuition of the Earth, was forgotten. This was a fall, but one that contained the capacity of resurrection.

Fifth Shrine: Great Nature

The fifth shrine is the Shrine of Great Nature. Its sign implies reconnection with the spiritual universe—with becoming aware of the movement of cosmic time and time-beings in the midst of human experience. Evolutionarily, it was the moment of the great religions, which structured mediumship from the elemental level all the way to the divine. The capacity for magic, healing, and ritual arose. The gods were named and relationships unfolded. Individuality developed in relation to the rhythmic flow of time, which embodied spirit beings. The veil of death was drawn across the world. Tombs, shrines to the ancestors, became places of worship and people began to construct dwellings over their dead.

Sixth Shrine: Blood

The sixth shrine is the Shrine of Blood. Blood is the medium of exchange, the threshold between the worlds. On the altars, now spread far and wide across the Earth, blood offering created the sacred. Blood ties dominated consciousness. Tribes and nations arose. Strife became the norm. With strife, and the omnipresent universal consciousness of war, came the recognition that blood held the essential powers of the self. Blood ensured continuity and preservation. It was understood to be the bearer of the self that circulated throughout the organism. Blood bore the ongoing work of creation into the generation of humanity through time. It carried memory—the memory of beginning and the journey of consciousness.

These cosmological elements provide the understanding of the prophecies of creation in the flow of time. They show the movement of spirit through these elemental fields that give rise to specific qualities in Super Nature and human beings. They are powers and laws that affect the manifestation of things and their transformation as well. They support how we communicate, how we perceive and cognize reality. The shrines support a wide range of medicine, substance that revitalizes and restores the integrity of the natural world.

REMOVING THE VEIL

The Veil protects the human being from outer forces. It is a state of consciousness that gives a human being the quality of freedom. As our own boundary the Veil determines the nature of the reality that we conceptualize. It supports the human being's initiative to cultivate free will for the purpose of self-development and autonomous self-expression. The Veil represents boundaries of the soul that can only be removed by inner experiences and intention. It is in essence our way of being free.

What comes into human life through sense perception is received by this veil, discerned and integrated into faculties of consciousness that prepare the human being for how to be. The Veil is our initiation threshold that opens and closes for the expansion of consciousness and for elevating the will forces toward deeper self-purpose. It mediates for us our consciousness in the world of the spirit and cultivates the will forces within the deeper regions of the human potential. Intention allows the Veil to be transparent, providing access to the creative forces that will, in time, create the outer world. At this threshold, understanding and agreement are forged out of one's own self-consciousness. This happens not because of anything from the outside but because of what we give freely of ourselves out of the awareness that the door of consciousness can only be opened from the inside.

10
THE VEIL

The new millennium brought into our collective human societies a deeper exploration of what is changing in our world. From the standpoint of Dagara cosmology the world was moving from a triple mineral year symbolized by the year 1999. The number nine represents the element of mineral, the power of memory, and the hidden language of the soul. The year 1999 symbolized this cosmological framework. It was a year empowered by the deep soul memory that we share as a collective world culture and what human beings had developed out of this shared awareness of time. The ending of that year meant that we were moving into another phase of who we are as human beings on the planet.

The way in which we use time is also affected by how we use numbers. Our calendars calibrate for us not so much the world of possibilities, where things that affect our lives lie beyond our reach and beyond our consciousness. Rather, our calendars help us decide for what is probable, what is most likely to happen. The year 1999 pointed not to the end of a millennium but to remembering what the millennium had cultivated in the development of soul and spirit consciousness.

By contrast, the year 2000, a year of the triple zero, was understood to be a year of triple earth, since zero designates and represents the element of earth. The natural earth and the elemental earth within each human being are activated to a higher valance. Earth is the element of home, of return to the inner authentic nature. It is the home of the self. The Earth is a source of abundance, generosity, and gifts. This signaled to the elders of the Earth shrines, in many African communities of memory, that it was time for radical ritual to unleash the outpouring of spiritual resources from the deeper recesses of the Earth. What is cultivated as the potential in the Earth for the development of humanity was now to be dispersed into the world. This triple earth year represented the highest potential field of transformation and the portal for initiating new agreements within the world.

In connection with this millennium change and the rituals that were to take place I went with Malidoma Somé to Burkina Faso. I was part of a group of four that was to participate in divination and rituals. We landed in Ghana for a connecting flight, but missed it. The next possible flight to Burkina Faso was four days later. This occurrence opened for us a block of unplanned time. After discussion, we decided that whatever had happened to give us these four days, we were going to use it in relationship to the purpose of our journey to Africa. We knew it had to do with ancestral memory and the shrine that was to be activated.

We checked into a hotel for the duration. On the second day, I woke very early; it was still dark. Thinking about the purpose of our trip, I began to write in my journal. I was awakened by impressions of the Middle Passage, by the deeper essence of the ancestral doorways opening toward the Great Waters. I was reflecting on what shaped Africa's destiny, and who I was, returning as a descendant of this place. I felt that

I was there to know something about myself, about the agreements I carry within me, and to understand what was bringing me back to Africa.

When I had finished writing in my journal, I showered and got dressed and went outside. Standing at the entrance of the hotel, observing the activity of the early morning, I noticed someone approaching. It was still dark and I couldn't make out who it was. A young man approached and asked if he could speak with me. He introduced himself as Ben. Then he said, "I was sitting on a stone close to my mother's home, trying to figure out what to do with my life. My grandfather told me to come to talk with you." He then said, "I must tell you my grandfather is dead." I replied, "It's okay."

He said that he had been praying to his grandfather, asking for help, when he heard his grandfather's voice telling him to look to the hotel. He looked and saw me standing there. Then his grandfather said, "Go to him and he will tell you what to do." I asked him what he wanted to know. He began to speak about what I had written in my journal an hour before. I was shocked. These were my thoughts, my questions, not his.

I stood in the silence looking at the dawning of this day as people moved into their daily routines—the shopkeepers arriving, children on their way to school. Traffic was moving back and forth between the everyday world and the world in which I was now standing, entering the deeper ground of the African way of life as I stood next to a stranger connected by the intimacy of thoughts shared by an ancestral reality.

Africa was more than the dust that filled the air as cars drove by, the sound of voices that called out greetings, the mundane busy-ness that overlooked what is always sacred and present as a space between human beings and nature, and between human beings and the spiritual world. The night had given me something, which this day was confirming. Ben and I stood there and talked while the sun came up. This experience was for me a confirmation that the ancestral world was trying to access this world in order to do its service. I also realized that I stood in what appeared to be darkness but I was being seen, not only by Ben's eyes but by the eyes of his grandfather. I had a new, deeper understanding of the concept of *sawubona*, "we see you." As we look for truth and as we call to the ancestral world to help in the fulfillment of our purposes, our eyes and the eyes of the ancestors become one, a way of seeing, a way of recognizing, a way of confirming. We become the doorways that enable the ancestral work to be done in the world.

The Doorway at Elmina

My experience with Ben led our group to decide to make the journey to Elmina, a city on the coast in Ghana. In Elmina, the Portuguese built the first fortress to hold captive Africans preparing for the journey of the Middle Passage. Elmina served as a threshold for what was to be the most radical change in the way of life for the African people. It launched an event that would last for more than three hundred years and involved the systematic removal of humanity from home, shrine, and culture.

Arriving in Elmina was like going back in time, into the distant memory of events that have shaped the nature of the world. Elmina remained connected to something that was unfinished. It was empty, yet it was filled with the cries and the pain of the human spirit. There was no way to prepare for the descent, literally and spiritually, into the dungeons that held captive the entire life of each person and destiny of a people. The presence of the ancestral world was palpable. We entered the building, going through the dungeons and holes where the Africans were held before being placed on the ships. I remember clearly the "door of no return." Standing in the dark, looking out at the water, I truly entered for the first time into the Mysteries of the ancestral world. We didn't say much to each other. The silence spoke loudly. We knew more than we could say.

On this day we had come to a place that served as a place of captivity and now had become an ancestral shrine holding within its stone walls the memory of everything that had occurred there, a great human and spiritual tragedy. I would continue to meditate on that doorway. I knew I would have to choose how to use this doorway, how to enter the ancestors' world in service to this memory, in service to what their lives had to endure. I was returning on their behalf to see again and to be seen as their legacy. It was a door of return, for I was a witness, not there in bondage, not there for enslavement, but to remember and to remove the veil so that we can see into the future created by this great sacrifice. It could not be in vain. The dark night is over. The light that enters this dungeon from the outside enters me. It is the light of a new age born out of the dark, still night of the ancestors longing for a heart that would understand and eyes that would see. The door remained open for me and I'm sure for others who asked—not why this happened—but now that it has happened, what must I do with the memory of it?

Finally we arrived in Burkina Faso. After settling in at Malidoma's home in Ouagadugu, the Capital, we continued our conversations about what we experienced in Ghana and what we were to do after arriving four days later than we had initially planned. As part of our preparation to go to the village of Dano we went to see a Dagara priest who practiced a form of divination using sand. The "sand-diviner" utilizes specially prepared sand into which he writes symbolic messages received through his spiritual faculties and relates to us what these messages say. Each of us had time to explore questions with him about our life, our initiation process, and the rituals ahead of us.

During my divination several things were revealed. First, the diviner shared an image of a blue room, a room dedicated to healing, a place to meet and work with people. He asked me if such a room existed and I replied no. He had seen it as a vision connected to my work. There was a reflection around my ancestors, particularly the ancestor that carried the medicine of the waters, the knowledge of the sacred nature of water, its potential to carry messages between the worlds and its use in healing. He told me of the role I had to bring the ancestral knowledge deeper into my family. I had to bring this knowledge to others who would ask for help in making contact with their ancestors. I inquired about a number of things that had to do with work, with the cosmological element of water. I asked about the rituals that I was to be a part of. After each of us had our turn with him and rituals were prescribed, we departed to prepare for the journey to the village of Dano.

When we arrived in Malidoma's village, we learned that rituals were being prepared for our group as well as for the whole community. One ritual led by the Chief of the Earth shrine was to coincide with similar rituals in other countries on the West Coast of Africa that are the sites of other Earth shrines. This particular ritual had not been done before. The ritual concerned the Middle Passage and the spiritual legacy of those who died in it. It was designed to end the great cycle of that initiation. It was designed to use the Earth shrine to change the destiny of those who were connected to that spiritual initiatory reality. The ancestral dead were being guided home. The veil between the worlds would be removed so that the ancestral forces could become accessible in the souls and spiritual lives of those for whom that sacrifice was made. With the changing of the millennium, these forces would serve the potential for new agreements in the world

The Chief of the Earth shrine in Dano was 110 years old. He invited us to the space where we started the ritual under a great tree. He told us that he was a child of seven when he saw the last group of slaves chained beneath this very tree. He didn't know where they were taken from that point but he shared his memory of seeing them bound under this great tree. We started the ritual that would last for several days. For me, the ritual signaled the work of the Seventh Shrine that was connected to my life and to the world in which I live. The sacrifice of this human blood, the cost of freedoms that were not visible at the time, somehow had to do with faith and with a new way of seeing.

I continued my study and practice within the framework of the Dagara cosmology, assisted and mentored by Malidoma and the diviners in the Dagara community in Burkina Faso. There were ever-increasing levels to this traditional practice of initiation and training as a diviner and priest. Malidoma had profound experience as a holder of this tradition. He had access and life experience within the Western cultural frameworks. His experience provided a very balanced context for exchange between us about the application of Dagara spiritual systems to the work that I was doing in the United States.

On my last visit with Baba Credo Mutwa, he had investigated the ritual forms that my initiation could take. After one such divination he told me of a spiritual vortex on the coast of California that would be an appropriate location for a ritual to align me with another phase of my destiny. This was an ancestral meridian running through a natural threshold connected to the waters of the Pacific. Noting that this was the closest meridian to my home, Credo identified it as suitable for an initiation process appropriate to my work in the United States. These energetic water corridors have served for certain water initiations in various ritual systems including the indigenous American initiation rites that relate to what was called the Gateway of the West, or the gate to the world of the dead, or the ancestors and the world of prophecy. Credo said that where the sun sets along the horizon of this great body of water lay a portal for the initiation that I was to undertake. Because Credo was unable to travel to provide assistance with doing the ritual, he asked me to consult Malidoma about facilitating it and noted that he would send instructions to support what must be done.

During my conversations with Malidoma about Credo's request, Malidoma shared that it would require elders with specific knowledge to open such a gateway and by himself it would be too large an undertaking. He then suggested that we start the preparation for this in his village in Dano, to enter through the *Kontomble* shrine a merger with the *Kontomble* medicine. We began our preparation with various divinations. After consulting the Kontomblé shrine, I was told the preparation had been made. The ancestors behind my destiny and the spiritual allies that assist my activity in the spiritual and physical world had prepared a process that was to be facilitated in Burkina Faso at the Kontomblé shrine. The preparation for this would take a full year and I was to engage this process in 2001.

In January of 2001 a group of us left the United States to further our studies and work in Burkina Faso. Arrangements had previously been made for a number of us to become aligned with the Kontomblé medicine, which meant a ritual initiation with the spiritual entities that provide a formal working paradigm to access various spiritual shrines and the ancestral world.

SEVENTH SHRINE: IMANI

The Seventh Shrine is the human experience borne out of sacrifice. It is what I recover of myself when no outer resources can be reached and I am therefore left to decide for what should be, what I must give, and who and what I am as a human being. I am free not because of what is or is not happening, but I am free by the nature of being human. My nature carries within it the predisposition to begin. Faith is the decision to begin to act as if my choice provides the seed for what will be. I permit myself to be the host of a future that is free, that can be created only by those who decide for it. Because of the way the future comes to the human being, it cannot be oppressed. It arrives as grace, a free space, a world of possibility into which I must decide. What I posit into that world of consciousness we call the future.

Through this action, I initiate an event that is prophetic, probable, and practical. It causes change to occur in confirmation with my will. Faith is an act of will aligning the highest in myself with the greatest good in the world. It is a summons of the forces of creation that supports what I decide and how I decide for it. These forces that are free of ego and self-interest are purposeful in their service and provide a rallying point for what I ask for.

Faith is the inner preparation to decide for the best when I am at my best, as a giver of the seed for what arises as new and free in our world. It is the consequence of the inner certainty of the primal intuition of truth, goodness, and beauty when it moves beyond the idea into the human will. I act from this space knowing that what I give supports something greater than myself.

11

IMANI

The Promised Land

When I went to Burkina Faso during January of 2001, I visited a little village on the outskirts of the capital city. I was invited by a friend to meet an elder there who was going to provide a divination for me. Approaching the village I saw a mosque and realized that this community was of the Islamic tradition that is a distinct part of West African life. I was greeted by the elder, who was the imam of the mosque and who, I had been told, used a very complex system of divination. After he had done some initial investigation of what lay behind my life and the connections to the spiritual world, he told me it was very important to take some further steps before I returned home.

He invited me into the mosque and asked me to stand by the door. As the elder spoke I relied upon my friend for translation. As we waited for the instructions, I observed that we were completely alone in the mosque. I learned that this mosque was 215 years old at that time and it was the site of one of the most sacred earth shrines in that area. This elder was the keeper of the knowledge of how to access those portals within the Earth.

When the elder appeared again, he began praying. Standing a few feet away and facing us, he asked us to wait until he told us to cross a corridor. He walked a few feet ahead of us and stopped. He turned and opened what appeared to be an energetic space. There was no visible activity, but he cautioned us to cross only after he told us to do so.

When we were instructed to cross I experienced an energetic change in my physical body. This process was repeated five times and each time the energetic change became more profound, more perceptible. It felt as if I were going deeper into the Earth or into a place where the air pressure was changing. There was no visible change in the structure of the building or the corridor in which we were walking. The doors and the walls remained as they were. The only noticeable change was in my perception of myself. I could feel the changes in my inner ear, and when we reached the central place that held the shrine I could hear an echo in my ear when I spoke. I was in a new experience, unfamiliar, very quiet and still.

Facing the shrine, the elder spoke another prayer and with the most profound humility asked permission to bring me forward to it. He then asked me to step forward and greet the shrine. He told me what to say, then he read my divination to the shrine. He asked permission to give me access to the shrine for the purpose of fulfilling what I had to do in the world. He committed to be a guide for this process and said that I would continue to communicate with him after my return home. We closed the ritual and returned to the main door. The process of closing the various thresholds, the reverse of our previous action, was done as we made our way out of the building.

The elder then created a medicine bath with herbs of various kinds and asked me to wash myself with it repeatedly before returning home to the United States. While I remained in the village I followed this and other protocols that he shared. He told me that within twelve days after returning home I would receive a message from the shrine clarifying my work in the world; I would hear spoken what my work was now to be. I returned home the following day to Los Angeles, reflecting profoundly on this experience and feeling strongly connected to the images of that place, the ritual, the shrine, and this particular elder.

Home again, I tried to return to the normal processes of my work, but the feeling that I had not left the inner space I visited in the shrine always interrupted it. Nevertheless, I did as much as I could do in the normal course of activity. During my daily meditations the words would come, "The children of Israel in the wilderness for forty years." There were no images, no visions, only the words. I asked myself again and again, "Why are these words coming to my mind?" It occurred to me that they might be a message from the shrine but I was not sure.

On the tenth day after my return, I received a phone call from my close friend and colleague Aqeela Shirell, the founder of the Community Self-Determination Institute (CSDI), a community based initiative for the gang truce intervention work in Watts. This was the first year in the life of this organization and Aqeela had asked me to serve as the chairman of its board of directors. Aqeela had acquired a building on the corner of 91st Street and Hooper in the community of Watts and had begun to redesign it to house the offices for CSDI. He had offered to provide a room for my office. Feeling that I didn't really need an office, I suggested instead a sanctuary, a place for healing and the conversations that could result in healing.

After months of construction some friends volunteered to paint the sanctuary. They decided to use a specific technique of applying color called *Lazure*. It took about three days to put the first layers of the glazes on the wall. While I was in Africa, they had made the decision to paint the sanctuary blue. When I returned and saw this blue room, I understood what the sand diviner's vision had foreseen. We had now created a place for this particular work to be made available.

In this sanctuary Aqeela and I were now sitting in conversation. He told me that we were invited to meet Minister Louis Farrakhan, the head of the Nation of Islam. The role of the Nation of Islam in the development of black cultural life has always been prominent from the time of its founding. It served to inspire strong leadership for the masses of black people who were loyal to other frameworks of religion and cultural and spiritual activism. The leaders, from the Honorable Elijah Muhammad to Malcolm X to Minister Louis Farrakhan advocated the complete freedom of black cultural and spiritual life within America. This cultural institution and its leadership were always seen as controversial and the aim of the service has often been misunderstood. Closer examination of the leaders' commitments shows that their collective purpose was to advocate for what was true and right for the liberation of the souls of black folks. Their advocacy for an active pro-black cultural development did not necessarily mean that they objected to the cultural positions of others.

Minister Farrakhan was coming to Los Angeles to meet with those involved in gang-intervention work, intending to lend support to us because of the high incidence of murders in the city over the previous few months. Minister Farrakhan was one whose reputation and vision could reach the young men in the streets. Consequently, he was able to influence the Peace Agreements that came together in various cities among rival gangs.

On the day of the meeting with Farrakhan, I arrived at work to meet with Aqeela at our sanctuary and offices in Watts. I noted that this was the twelfth day of my return from Burkina Faso. I shared with him that every morning my meditations were interrupted with the words, "the children of Israel in the wilderness for forty years." When he asked me what I thought it meant, I shared with him what I knew of the story of the journey of Moses in preparation for entry into what was called the Promised Land after the new covenants had been made between the children of Israel and God.

When we arrived we entered the conference center and sat around a large table. There were about thirty of us, mostly young men and women, when Minister Farrakhan arrived. We introduced ourselves and then he opened with a prayer. He said, "I would like to choose as my theme for our conversation, a theme from the Bible—the children of Israel in the wilderness for forty years." When he spoke the words it rang loudly in my ears and more loudly in my soul, for I knew I was hearing something beyond this moment we were sharing. I felt that the world had turned. Something had entered the room and me. A deeper memory was beginning to unfold. I glanced at Aqeela who was watching me and mouthing the words, "You were just talking about this." I responded, "I can't believe that I'm hearing this."

Aqueela and I then knew that this was a message, an important step toward what we had gathered to do. Minister Farrakhan said, "I'm now 70 years old and my life's work was to bring healing to our people." He went on to say that the violence that was taking hold of our young people could not be transformed without deeper agreements. This was generational work, he felt, that reached beyond his time, but he noted that there were those in the room who must help this process unfold by indicating the ways to bring these new covenants and agreements into our communities.

Farrakhan reflected on his life's work, using the analogy of the sojourn of the Israelites under bondage in Egypt and their pathway to redeem their spiritual legacy. He drew a parallel with the African experience in America, our bondage, enslavement, and emancipation, the journey through the American wilderness for something of our own making, as an agreement to the sacrifice made for this generation to inherit. Minister Farrakhan stood as an elder holding open a veil, revealing what was at stake.

He talked from his heart and pleaded for a continued effort to save the lives of our people, of our youth. As he reflected on the ancestral world, he petitioned those in my generation and younger to step beyond the veil of self-doubt, self-hate, and violence to embrace the legacy that awaits us promised by faith and anointed by struggle. He provided the most intimate context for understanding who we must become so that this promise can be fulfilled. As he shared his profound story, his insights into this biblical passage, I received the ancestral prophecy of seeing what was behind the forty years in which the struggle for meaning was happening for us.

Reflecting upon this experience, I realized that Martin Luther King Jr. had also used the term *Promised Land* as a prophetic expression of our collective work here in America. So I began to prepare to understand the path leading to this Promised Land.

The story of the children of Israel in the wilderness examines a fundamental human initiation process, one that relies on faith and a multigenerational succession of practice in bringing the soul to a new state of fulfillment for a particular world reality. The nature of the soul is to create both the consciousness and the agreements that allow the human individual and his fellow men to stand free.

The covenant between the Creator and the people of Israel concerned laws for the cultivation of practical disciplines required to cross the boundaries of the soul, referred to as the Jordan River. To examine initiation, its progression, and ultimately what it produces for the human being, one must understand the first phase of the initiation process. Often this can be seen as a separation from a normative state of reality, a change in what we know as certain, which turns us toward our dilemma and a search for meaning.

> *Forty years constitutes a time frame of two generations, phases of life that put human beings in a relationship to child, parent, and grandparent. This threefold nature of the human family, this generational picture constitutes the lens of what we must know about our inheritance in order to step through the veil. The collective work within a culture requires an agreement between at least three existing generations for the appropriate understanding of what each holds in the soul for the bridge of return to be created.*

Forty years in the Kabbalistic tradition represents the cycle of initiation, the integration of the laws that are in the soul, to be remembered and to be called forth. It is a measure of initiation that supports the free will and the creation of the covenant for the world in which one lives and serves. In the teachings of theosophy, forty years represents the fourth ray of initiation, harmony through conflict. The symbolic nature of the forty-year cycle speaks to what must be accomplished within the human being for earthly service to remove the forces of doubt and fear as we establish our mental and psychic creative intention for being fully awake. It is also the opportunity to dedicate these awakened soul forces toward the maturation of the human society and the renewing of our relatedness to the world of the spirit. The Earth is to be a host for the harmony of the spheres that lies beyond the natural expressions of reality, and the human being is in service to this purpose.

As part of the initiation process of the forty-year cycle a covenant is created. A covenant is an innate capacity that is inherited, created, and initiated within the human being for a specific task. It is a superconsciously occurring framework that becomes conscious through the application of disciplines—mental, psychic, and moral. They support what we do in the transformation of life. Ultimately a covenant becomes our deed and our legacy. In the world of manifestation we decide for the release of our creative free forces. A covenant is freely made, because it requires human beings to give not just for their own benefit. It requires us to give to the future that will come out of what they do.

A covenant is an act that posits in the world something beyond self-interest, often attracting or relying on the contributions of higher spiritual entities. It is never an agreement between us as human beings alone. It involves the natural and supernatural laws lying within the realms of human destiny for the purpose of human development. Both nature and the spiritual world respond when, through ritual, we invite the spiritual entities' participation in our daily affairs. A covenant is sacred because it stands above and beyond the individual self-interest. It sustains our discipleship to our highest development. It sustains the collected striving for agreements that continuously free the human being from his own limitations. It renews our capacity to be related. It renews our capacity to find common frameworks for shared awareness. In this covenant we renew our capacity to commune with nature for the continued balancing of the ecology that sustains human and planetary life.

Seventh Shrine: Imani

The African presence in America required an individual and collective effort to overcome the forces of exile and persecution. The willpower of African Americans was aimed at strengthening the spiritual capacities of seership that connected them to their ancestral and spiritual life. This inner faculty became more active in the development of capacities that streamed into the new cultural reality. Music, technology, natural, and spiritual scientific discoveries emerged from the Africans' creative inner life. *Overcoming* was a practice of recovering their inner seeing, their second sight. It became the Seventh Shrine, Imani. Imani is faith, the inner preparation to decide for a particular future out of one's own experience of freedom.

The cultural time in which we find ourselves is a time of radical transition. Major changes are occurring in every system—cultural, economic, ecological and spiritual. We humans are being brought to a threshold not just to fix the systems, but also to create a sustainable future. We are brought to this threshold to create an awareness of the deeper laws that lie behind the human creativity and the natural spiritual worlds. The power of imani is to ask the question—how do we prepare ourselves to be a giver in the world? The most remarkable thing to know about yourself is your predisposition to give—to know of the potential to create out of nothing; to create yourself as a thinking being; to be willing to communicate with other human beings, above and beyond the definitions of good and evil; to love another human being as a part of one's own future. We are essentially a power of communication deeply exteriorizing our inner faculties—those of understanding, truth, and love. We are exteriorizing life, love, and will. This is the human process of transformation.

Imani is an Indaba

Imani is an *indaba*, an inner dialogue that clarifies purpose. It is the higher intention of our hearts, the cognitive frameworks of our language. Our communication is an event structured by the super-conscious being of the human spirit. But we must be willing to say what we know through inner cognition and bring it into our speaking. It would be hard to understand what we can agree about without this inner experience. This inner dialogue reveals a source of consciousness. This inner dialogue guides the human attention to the intentional level of what he must speak to support the outer dialogue.

This process of *Imani* initiates the human being into the self-consciousness that knows itself as the speaker, the inner creative utterance of what becomes thought, speech, and action. It is a movement from the seed of life in the inner sanctuary, into the fruit of life. *Imani* is the whole gesture or the fulfillment of consciousness from its inner predisposition to create a deed out of nothing. This first principle of the Earth shrine allows an unprejudiced acceptance of the world. We must create the same gesture in a social sense for the other human being. We must create a sanctuary in our own heart–mind before that person can communicate what has never been communicated.

The Story of Elvonzo

A few months following this profound journey to a new understanding of our work in Los Angeles, I was heading into the city for a meeting. It was 7:30 in the morning when I arrived at the city center. I was early for the appointment I had that morning. While driving I experienced the thought that I should go to the sanctuary. The call was so urgent that I got off the freeway, turned around, and drove seven miles back to the office.

When I arrived, one staff member was there and asked why I was there so early. Explaining that I was just stopping by, I went to the sanctuary and sat for a few moments in stillness to discern what had brought me there. When no one else arrived within thirty minutes, I decided to leave. As I was walking out the door, a telephone call came for me. The person on the other end of the line was calling to see if I was there. I realized in that moment that this was why I had come to the sanctuary. I invited him over to meet with me and told him to come as soon as he could and that I would go to a meeting and return. Before I left the office the person with whom I had the appointment that morning called and canceled, so I waited at the office for this new encounter.

Elvonzo came through the door. I knew him through the work that he did with our organization involving transitioning from gang life into a more healing personal and social arrangement. He participated in our gang intervention work that required individuals to remain active in their own development. We had never met in an intentional way so we did not really know each other. This was to be our first conversation.

I invited him into the sanctuary and shared a little bit about what I do within my practice. He looked at me and asked if he could tell me more of what was happening with him. I told him I was completely open and willing to hear. Elvonzo told me that the night before he was thrown into a conflict that he thought could only be resolved with violence. He had reached a limit in his capacity to tolerate the overwhelming stress of living within violence and yet not being able to fully protect himself.

The rules of the street were such that he could not live without being pulled into the situations that put him at risk of being harmed or bringing harm to others. While he was contemplating his course of action, he was interrupted by the thought of calling the office to see if I was there. He said he heard about the things I did for others. Now he felt compelled to seek my help for reasons that were not quite clear to him. While we were talking, several other people called to cancel appointments with me. My day was now completely free to host this conversation space, this *indaba*, and what would turn out to be this ritual with Elvonzo.

We met for six hours, talking about many layers of Elvonzo's life, the hardships of childhood, the experiences in gangs, and his struggle to find meaning within the world. I asked him one question, "Do you have a dream?" I was asking about a deeper inspiration toward some future goal. He replied, "No, but I have a nightmare, one that occurs frequently." I asked him to share what he could of the nightmare. He replied that he thought he was going to die, because in the recurring dream he saw himself in a coffin at his own funeral. Everything around his life was falling apart to such an extent that he thought he was not going to live and, regardless, he didn't want to live this way. When I asked him if there were people in his life that he loved enough to keep him alive, people who could support his aim to serve, he said, "No."

It became quite clear to me that Elvonzo was indeed at risk of dying at any moment. He lived in a high-risk community. He was 24 years old, a typical age for death of young men involved in gangs. I asked if he was willing to decide for another way of life and find a way to transform this fate. He said he was willing to see if something could work.

I invited several staff members to come into the sanctuary and be part of this exercise of co-creating with Elvonzo an agreement for a possible future. Aqeela and several others who had known him since he was a boy were present to support this process. I asked each of them to share something that could be a source of inspiration, something he could take into himself to help him realize that he was not alone. I knew he was uncomfortable with the fact that it was no longer a conversation between him and me. He did not want to share his vulnerability in a group setting. I guided the process, trusting that every additional witness further assured the success of the ritual.

After each person had contributed a memory, I asked the group to be with Elvonzo in silence for a moment and then to leave him alone. I asked him to decide what he wanted his future to be. He couldn't decide completely on all the various levels of possibility because of his deep fear that he might not live. So I asked him if he would allow me to visualize a future for him and to hold that picture. After he agreed and this process of visualization was completed, he lit a candle to dedicate this future for himself. The flame of decision was symbolized by the awakening of his own intention for what would come into his life. The flame is a light that illuminates the path that leads from doubt to insight. It is a flame within the human heart that reawakens the dream and the will to live. He closed the ritual with the acknowledgement that something new was possible and that he should prepare every day to meet this new possibility. I asked him to come to the office as often as he could so that we could reinforce this intention. He did so for a few weeks.

Upon returning to Los Angeles following a trip abroad, I learned that Elvonzo had been shot. I was told that he had been hospitalized and that he was now home. I knew that he had anticipated this event, but I was surprised to hear that he was okay. I then thought to myself that the shooting must not have been serious because he was at home after only a couple of days in the hospital. I went directly to see him. Opening his apartment door, he looked at me with surprise. For a moment we stood in a state of silence. He invited me into the apartment. We sat again in silence. I asked him what happened.

Elvonzo told me that he was on his way to get lunch one afternoon with some friends, not very far from the housing community where he lived in Jordan Downs. As he arrived, a car pulled up and two individuals shot him. He was hit seven times in the chest. He collapsed on the ground His friends tried to resuscitate him. The paramedics were called. He was rushed to the hospital. On the way to the hospital, he heard them pronounce him dead. He began to remember the ritual. He remembered his intention to live. He was able to see the sanctuary. He was able to see the process we went through in the ritual. He remembered lighting the candle. He remembered making a commitment to live. After a moment he returned to what he sensed was the feeling of his body. He regained consciousness. When the ambulance arrived at the hospital he was rushed into surgery.

During surgery, Elvonzo flatlined again. He then experienced the forces of his heart awakening and growing stronger. As this happened he sensed a presence of a being of light and a being of love filling up his heart. He again regained consciousness. Finding vital signs, the medical team continued the surgery to remove the bullets from his body. After they had taken out six of the bullets he flatlined a third time. While they tried to resuscitate him, Elvonzo observed his family and friends who had arrived at the hospital to be with him. He remembered the dream of his funeral. All the feelings of being separated from his family came back to him. Elvonzo then realized that he wanted to live and he wanted to love.

He came back to his body. His vital signs were returned. The doctors discontinued the surgery, leaving one of the bullets inside his body.

After sharing this story, Elvonzo looked at me and asked, "What do you think happened?" I was very surprised by what he had told me. I replied that this was a very complex spiritual experience. I couldn't say much about it. I was grateful that he was alive. I was grateful that he had decided to live his life. We sat for a few moments in silence. I thought about the things he had shared. He showed me the surgical scars and the wounds with the sutures. I was amazed that he was physically able to stand and to share this story. Something profound had entered his life and his body. There was a deep strength and confidence in him.

I visited Elvonzo throughout the recovery process over the next few weeks until he regained enough strength to return to work. This incident became a turning point in his life and allowed for expansion in the relationships with his family. It provided a context for another pathway of learning about how he could be himself in spite of the circumstances of the world. The events introduced new inner experiences, uniting his will forces with the work that he must now do in the world. Elvonzo became an active mentor with our organization and began to formulate processes to support young men in stepping out of violence. He still lives in Los Angeles and is committed to the development of young people and the peace process in Watts.

I remembered being told that the Seventh Shrine would be accessed through dialogue, that questions would be raised about the possibilities of our life and the life circumstances we choose. It is the fate, knowledge, and power of this mission to know what is probable and decide for it. Elvonzo's experience confirmed access to the shrine—the power of agreement two or more human beings can co-create. I learned that the shrine lives within human relationships. Our future is created by it. It is opened by faith. This event became the first intentional way of working with this knowledge. This event added to my own development and learning about the Seventh Shrine.

PART III
RETURNING HOME

Empathy

What the empathy cultivates is a love for how to serve the world's future, which is simultaneously evolving in front of them as a witness of the other.

12

ACCESSING THE SEVENTH SHRINE

The use of the word shrine in this context of *Imani* speaks not to a thing given and established as tradition. The word shrine refers to the inner process of what individuals give to themselves to remain free. It is a human act realized by the utilization of our inner life—the light of understanding and wisdom and the love of our free disposition from which we can and should decide. This path, as an initiation path, brings the human being constantly toward the threshold of asking: How must I be so that you can be free? How do I host the freedom of the other, the development of the other, and the greater truth of the other?

This act cannot be compelled by civil law, nor by theological or philosophical doctrine. It is what human beings can do when we utilize what's truly human and become self-attentive as a source for what becomes reality. Reality is never finished. What appears as given by nature and culture comes into the human life and is augmented by our consciousness. Our consciousness determines the level of reality that can be created out of what is given. Consciousness is reality. This process of ascension is not to leave the world but to integrate it into oneself, participate in it as a co-creator, and release its new potential.

The Seventh Shrine can be observed in many cultural streams, again not as a tradition, but as a capacity to act when the circumstances require an act of faith. What is awakened in the human being in a time of difficulty is the predisposition to make contact with the spiritual world, the invisible guidance within one's destiny. We meet, daily in our lives, circumstances that bring us to this threshold of initiation. It does not make us less human to falter, to question the circumstances of life—in fact it is the human thing to do. In order to cross into this territory of the soul where we rely on possibilities unknown, the human mind must give its authority over to the spiritual recesses that create a new Knowledge, thus giving a new certainty to what we had decided without evidence.

The historical experience of slavery and what followed after emancipation was an Initiation. It was a preparation for a new capacity within the life of a group of people. It was to influence the destiny of a nation. The social, spiritual striving inherent in the souls of black folks brought to bear on America the cultivated indigenous wisdom of what this land carried for peace. This love for the future became deeply experienced within the cultural–spiritual faculties that this initiation awoke in black people. It was their task to stand against the social difficulties of their time. This task was to communicate to others what they were inwardly aware of—that freedom is a shared reality. Someone must choose to be free in order to support the other to be free.

This decision, to act out of freedom beyond self-interest or gain, supports the cultivation of a faculty that guides us toward insight to certain spiritual truths that are bestowed upon the human heart and mind as a grace. We are made free by it, not from sacrifice or challenge. We are made free to increase our capacity to carry what we do carry in light of the times in which we live. We are hosting the future so that it may enter our world through us. This expression of life that is sourced beyond the temporal can be accessed for the strengthening of the will to live.

Living is not just a biological state. It is a state of causing change to occur in confirmation with this innate human nature of knowing how to choose to be free. Change is reflected in the outer world most profoundly when it is enacted inwardly to the degree that we stand firmly in that truth: What is created out of this inner law of life lived. What is lived intentionally in the heart space. What is lived in the moral and mental space of the human creative process is now made manifest for the benefit of the world. It becomes not my will but thy will, a service for something beyond self.

Light in this context refers to the capacity of the human being to create understanding. Understanding is not given. It does not come assigned in the texts we read, in the language we hear, or in the images we see. The light of understanding is a self-endowed realization—when we are able to transform these particular qualities of the perceptible world and add to it our own attention and intention to become "a knower of what I behold."

Understanding reveals and illuminates the human consciousness to itself. It allows us to recognize that what appears as the world enters our awareness as incomplete possibilities. When understanding occurs, we create a specific context that places our knowing firmly into the human experience. At the same time it builds a capacity for us to communicate more intentionally with others in the world. Understanding is light and as we are lighted we become a light unto others. We share with them our insight not to persuade or correct but to communicate, to share, and to participate in what is mutually a deep human experience. The possibility for shared understanding is the reason why we communicate, not for the sake of argument of what is right and what is wrong, what is good and what is evil, but that we may find meaning to trust each other's word, to forgive each other's mistakes, and to create the agreements around what we can share.

Love is the process that redeems what is lost in ourselves and in the world. Love unites the discontinuities into a sphere of mutual expression of the same unity. It recovers from the unconscious aspects of the soul. It recovers the hidden and lost forces that fall into unconsciousness when we do not act out of freedom. The ideal striving of human intellectual life is not for the purpose of some perfected utopia. The ideal for the human being is a strengthening of the faculty of love—a search for meaning when the spheres of knowledge or the conventions of society are no longer adequate. Love gives us a way when knowledge is limited, circumstances unsure, and the task heavy.

Love is an agreement that reestablishes contact with the source—the source of will and the source of life itself. Love mediates the fields of possibility and the fields of probability. Love draws in all those spiritual entities that are willing to give without any self-interest. They are willing to participate in human destiny in a gesture of service and sacrifice. They aid us freely in our development. They are witnessing strength to us and they direct our sensibilities toward the future.

In the initiation process, after the separation from the familiar, one experiences exile. It might take the form of an individual being in prison, ill, or divorced from a significant relationship. Being alone is a state of experiencing a threshold of change. Initiation is present when we are on the threshold of change. Our psychic life puts before us a path. A path is a process of development for inner capacities to support outer tasks. A path defines character and clarifies destiny. A path provides the person the social significance for right livelihood. Our path is a call to find ever-deeper intentions for living out the inner dreams and aspirations through outer work and service, to offer something greater than oneself.

The Act of Imani in Mentorship

The human being lives in a world that's constantly changing. The constant factor is change. When we encounter an individual we encounter a radical experience that we often don't acknowledge, two individual realities. We recognize that we are separate due to some factor that we don't completely understand. When people seek mentorship, they are looking for a conversation and relationship to correct a process of being isolated from the sense of unity of a shared reality. The mentor, if prepared to serve this relationship, provides the right framing questions for the individual to reflect. The feeling of separation is an awareness of an inner sense that I need to communicate. Often the first question is: What's happening? This provides a context for the person to describe the immediate circumstances. They may describe the crisis they are currently in by sharing the physical or emotional pain, the psychological stress, the financial crisis, the violent relationship, and other possibilities of emotional, mental, and social conflict. This allows for an assessment of the immediate risks—the exploration of how to safeguard the individual from further losses.

This assessment provides the first framework for knowing how prepared the mentor might be for dealing with this specific individual and their life's circumstances. Depending on the risk factors involved, the mentor can decide whether she or he needs additional resources through another person or another agency to help the individual.

The next step in the framing of the mentorship conversation is to find a timeline of when these things that are affecting the person's life begin. Depending on the age of the person requesting mentorship, the mentor can assess to some degree the significance of the psychological wound that this person might be carrying, the impact on certain emotional and mental abilities, the internalization of the trauma and difficulties and their capacity of will to accept or resist help. The timeline also supports the mentor in establishing another level of availability for what will be required in serving the individual.

Another step of assessment is the relational context of the person's life. Who or what are the causes, whether true or not, of the dilemma that the person is in? What factors of this crisis were caused by people—beginning with those that are known and moving further out into what people sometimes call they, an unknown human factor particularly characteristic of the social space and time in which the person lives. This second assessment gives the mentor a way of knowing strategies for shaping the conversation. It gives help to the individual to build the language to advocate their own truth. It helps them negotiate how they change their relationship to those who are violating them or causing the conflict.

The mentor can further investigate the resiliency of the individual. How prepared are they for the change that can be made? It is the resilient capacity that is mentored in a crisis-oriented mentorship situation. This gives the first framework for understanding the separation and dilemma stage of an initiation experience.

Some forms of mentorship approach another threshold, the threshold of the gift. Here the youth observes a specific quality in the mentor that illuminates in them the need to know what the mentor knows and what the mentor does to overcome certain obstacles. Their deeper interest is to know what supported the mentor to be in the place where they now are. Their deeper interest is to imagine a similar future for themselves. Here the conversation is about the gift that provides a source of inspiration for the perfecting of the gift in the youth that's being mentored. Sometimes it's called polishing the gift or honoring the gift. This can move through stages of development where the person being mentored can apprentice, where other attributes of the gift can be further enhanced and utilized for a particular path.

Divination

> "*There is a power in love to divine another's destiny better than that other can and through heroic encouragement hold him to his task.*"—Ralph Waldo Emerson

Mentorship is a capacity to be guided by love and the wisdom of one's own lived experiences, to aid in the guidance of another human being's life potential. Divination is the capacity to see beyond one's self-interest into the life circumstances of another person. This inner free force and the intelligence that love brings into human consciousness support it. Divination takes many different cultural forms. One universal quality of divination is the capacity to love. Here we encounter a process that allows the human being to give and to receive a substance that makes other levels of communication possible.

Divination allows us to host the imagination of what it will take for someone to be free. It draws on the inspiration of the destiny forces in our own lives. It draws on the guiding intelligences in the spiritual world to support our particular efforts in aiding the life of a fellow human being. It gives us the incentive to carry the responsibility for a human being until they can carry it for themselves. Divination is a higher art of communication that draws on the worlds of possibility—the creative potential to bring into the now what will serve as a foundation for change and healing. Every mentor that orients the heart toward service of another person's life experiences divination—a deep clear way of understanding and knowing what the person is attempting to communicate. Mentors become capable of reading the character of the person, their innate struggles, and the pathway of destiny. Divination can be understood as a presence of a clear knowing that is sourced by the divine mind and the powers of love. Divination is the nature and expression of the spirit.

Capacities

Mentorship is a capacity in us when we are called forth by someone in need of a particular human relationship. A mentor is chosen and this choice places the mentor in receivership of certain spiritual influences. A mentor receives through the spirit of inspiration an awareness to draw on cultivated soul capacities in themselves to serve the people that seek mentorship.

Knowledge

A fundamental part of human development is developing the capacity to know. To be able to cultivate knowledge serves a person in being able to release creative forces into one's life and into the world. Being a knower of the nature of reality and of human possibilities is a critical process in mentorship. The mentor helps the individual to become a knower of the processes of life, which begins with being able to become self-aware. They begin to be able to formulate strategies of developing specific structures and bodies of knowledge. It is through mentorship that people are able to bring their historical experiences into current awareness. This becomes specific knowing. Every experience that we undergo in life provides us a quality of knowledge. This knowledge then influences our development—the various disciplines that allow us to further enhance our life and contribute to the creation of a shared reality. The capacity of crossing the boundary of the soul, whereby individuals feel themselves to be exiled, begins with the capacity of knowledge. It orients the mind and strengthens the capacity to deal with uncertainty. The development requires three areas of capacity building.

Abilities

A fundamental ability in human life is the ability to communicate. The purpose of our communication is to enhance our relationship with others for the purpose of strengthening our social will and consciousness. This human social striving leads the individual to a sense of self-sufficiency as well as being able to contribute to the wellbeing of the other. The ability to give is nurtured by the inner knowing that the individual carries within himself or herself a gift. Mentorship aims to cultivate awareness of this gift and to be able to create the necessary social strategies that allow individuals to bring their gifts into the world. Mentoring, the ability to communicate and to give, supports both the independence and the interdependence of a human life. The aim is to cultivate the capacity to negotiate conflicts and isolation. The aim is to support the person being in community. Social life is enhanced through this ability to contemplate, to aspire, and to participate in various levels of co-creative activity.

Sacrifice

The next level, which I think is most crucial, is where mentorship becomes a capacity to make a sacrifice, a genuine expression of a freedom that does not require knowledge, ability, or the other person to give before we give. A genuine sacrifice, which means to make sacred, is to be able to place oneself in the place of being a witness for something new to happen because "I" am giving freedom to it. It does not require knowledge or abilities. It is an act that a human being is capable of doing, when we are unable to find specific reference points for why "I" should act. We call it "faith." But it is a preparation that one does within oneself for an absolute place of beingness, when we are ready for the highest level of our own truth. There is wisdom in the soul that knows how to sacrifice—the wisdom in the self that knows how to step out of what's given or what's known, and to be a true witness for another level of possibility. This is so powerfully renewing—when we are left with no option but to give at that level.

Agreement

Agreement is the human capacity to hold an openness for the other, to reach a place of shared understanding for what can become reality. Agreement is the inner disposition for a person to take a stand for the greatest possible good. Agreement in this framework of mentorship does not mean a contract. It is how we relate to each other's inner human nature—what holds the predisposition of perfecting consciousness and reality. The tradition of *indaba* and in this case mentorship investigates what human beings must know, must understand, and must trust in themselves to be able to substantiate the creative acts that they can bring forth. Healing is a quality of agreement when inwardly we restore the balance that gives us optimum wellbeing.

Consciousness brings the human being into agreement with the worlds of nature and the worlds of spirit when we are able to cultivate deeper understanding of these laws. Human relationships are shaped by agreements in order for these processes to bring forth the creative human potential. Our language capacity carries within it the ability to understand and to further create inner and outer agreements for how to share the world in which we collectively live. An agreement serves as a foundation for individual and mutual aspiration for higher achievements within the world and attainments within the inner processes of life.

Accessing the Seventh Shrine leads us home. Community is the space that initiation guides a person to. The initiated heart–mind, the awakened self turns toward a relationship for the completion of the initiatory exercise. Ultimate initiation is about communicating into the world what is strengthened and cultivated within oneself. Community is the homecoming, the arrival, and the meeting place. Having been lost, abandoned, mistreated, or forgotten, our path leads us home through our inner meaning, giving free will to participate in the communal expression of life, liberty, and the pursuit of happiness. What we find in the world is directly proportional in our selves.

"I am happy to join with you today in what will go down in history as the greatest demonstration for freedom in the history of our nation.

Five score years ago, a great American, in whose symbolic shadow we stand today, signed the Emancipation Proclamation. This momentous decree came as a great beacon light of hope to millions of Negro slaves who had been seared in the flames of withering injustice. It came as a joyous daybreak to end the long night of their captivity.

But one hundred years later, the Negro still is not free; one hundred years later, the life of the Negro is still sadly crippled by the manacles of segregation and the chains of discrimination; one hundred years later, the Negro lives on a lonely island of poverty in the midst of a vast ocean of material prosperity; one hundred years later, the Negro is still languishing in the corners of American society and finds himself an exile in his own land.

So we've come here today to dramatize a shameful condition. In a sense we've come to our nation's capital to cash a check. When the architects of our republic wrote the magnificent words of the Constitution and the Declaration of Independence, they were signing a promissory note to which every American was to fall heir. This note was the promise that all men, yes, black men as well as white men, would be guaranteed the unalienable rights of life, liberty, and the pursuit of happiness.

It is obvious today that America has defaulted on this promissory note insofar as her citizens of color are concerned. Instead of honoring this sacred obligation, America has given the Negro people a bad check; a check that has come back marked 'insufficient funds.' We refuse to believe that there are insufficient funds in the great vaults of opportunity of this nation. And so we've come to cash this check, a check that will give us upon demand the riches of freedom and the security of justice."

—Martin Luther King Jr., "I Have a Dream"

13

THE PROPHECY OF MARTIN LUTHER KING JR.

This speech given in 1963 by Dr. Martin Luther King Jr. as part of the greatest demonstration for freedom in the history of our nation represented a call to humanity to make an agreement about what constitutes freedom. Given on the steps of the Lincoln Memorial, the speech holds more than the symbolic gesture of simply being in the shadow of Lincoln. The monument itself is a testimony to a relationship and a prophetic agreement about the destiny of blacks in America. Lincoln, as the signer of the Emancipation Proclamation, designated the authority of the State to suspend its political and social policies against the freedoms inherent in the lives of black people.

Beyond the political distinction held in the documents of the Emancipation Proclamation as well as the Constitution of the United States, are principles carried by the various groups of people who would have to work out through their own collective spiritual strivings the agreements that would constitute a nation under shared ideals. Policy by itself could not integrate these freedoms even though they required the authority of the state to acknowledge those rights. The freedom that was to be cultivated in the United States is not a political freedom but a cultural spiritual awareness of what the place carries for people to be able to share. The indigenous people knew that the nature of this land was such that it could not be conquered. It was never conquered. Those who took political control of the resources of the land, the people of the land, and the slaves brought to labor on the land—were now being forced to see the true nature of America. The true nature of America is that it is a place of liberty, a place that gives people their voice and their future beyond the political constraints and economic hardships.

Those who held political office were rooted in the knowledge of the Rosicrucian mandate to create a nation–state for the possibility for bringing into the age of humanity the political and economic frameworks that would support the higher aims of human life. Lincoln's knowledge of what blacks carried as a soul potential for this nation—the support of the unity of the States—reinforced the signing of this Proclamation. Dr. King articulated that the people had gathered to cash a check. He was speaking of a covenant, a written promissory note that held in it an agreement between the State and the people to pursue a path of development of the unalienable rights of Constitutional Law and human nature. It is within our nature to be free and this nature was called forth in the Emancipation Proclamation for the souls of black folks.

One hundred years after this Proclamation the full consciousness of this freedom had not been achieved due to the delay of the appropriate political and social measures necessary for affording blacks access to civil society—the freedom to participate in the agreements for the utilization and shared intention of their collective human potential.

A society is formed through social ritual when people see in each other the potential within themselves and formulate agreements, strategies, and relationships for the fulfillment of this inner potential. Laws designed to protect the agreements in civil society create a state. The march on Washington was a procession toward this monument of freedom, toward the memory of the Emancipation Proclamation, and toward the capital of the State to remind governing authorities of their responsibility to the civil, social, and spiritual development of a people.

It was also a call to those who embody the striving for this freedom to utilize what Dr. King called the soul forces, the moral methods of nonviolent protest to develop the expression of this inner life. On one level it was a protest against the state for its betrayal of this promissory note. On the other hand it was a procession and ritual to remind each other of the covenant that can only be realized by the inner exploration of what constitutes human nature and the purpose of life.

The dream that he articulated was rooted in the nature of this land, the mountaintops that he referenced from which freedom rings. He spoke to the inner capacity of human beings to agree beyond paradigms of belief, beyond the inheritance of race and class. His vision was for the human spirit to become self-conscious and to be dedicated to making a world that could be shared. He said that the year 1963 was not an end but a beginning and one must ask, "The beginning of what?" It was not the beginning of a Civil Rights Movement but the initiation of the use of the words "I have a dream" to place within the psyche of our nation the key words of the age to which humanity must awake to the prophetic nature to see into the stars, to see into the cosmos, to see into the soul and into one another the future. These few words give expression to the Gnostic tradition out of which Dr. King's legacy and practice grew, the mental and spiritual and moral use of the Word to decide for a distinct reality. He knew that one could call forth a reality by saying it. He knew what was probable knowing human nature and the laws of the spirit.

Journey to Memphis

In 2005 I took a journey to Memphis to explore what had been laid as the foundation of Martin Luther King Jr.'s vision, which he articulated the night before he was killed. In his speech "I've Been to the Mountaintop," he referenced a change that was occurring in the world. He began by reflecting on the possibility of the soul seeing the various turning points in human history when new soul powers entered human powers, entered consciousness, and gave human beings civilization. Beginning with the ancient Egyptian civilization, he painted a picture as if he were asked what age he would like to live in, given all that had been achieved in the world. He stated that he would choose exactly where he had been born, the time and place. Dr. King's complete acceptance of his initiation was symbolically demonstrated in this review of history leading to this threshold of change. He understood that birth constitutes something more powerful when we situate our will directly into it and discover the purpose for which we were born. He laid before us the example of purposefully being exactly where we are. He spoke of a change happening in the world, happening in Memphis, and happening in the people. He acknowledged in some strange way that people are responding to this inner freedom to call forth in themselves and call forth in their movement the soul forces that have been carried over from age to age, from generation to generation, from culture to culture. He explained that here in Memphis was a point where we have to see beyond what was given, into the promise we must make as a spiritual agreement, for what was now possible.

> But I wouldn't stop there. Strangely enough, I would turn to the Almighty, and say, "If you allow me to live just a few years in the second half of the twentieth century, I will be happy." Now that's a strange statement to make, because the world is all messed up. The nation is sick. Trouble is in the land. Confusion all around. That's a strange statement. But I know, somehow, that only when it is dark enough, can you see the stars. And I see God working in this period of the twentieth century in a way that men, in some strange way, are responding—something is happening in our world. The masses of people are rising up. And wherever they are assembled today, whether they are in Johannesburg, South Africa; Nairobi, Kenya; Accra, Ghana; New York City; Atlanta, Georgia; Jackson, Mississippi; or Memphis, Tennessee—the cry is always the same—"We want to be free."

The Lorraine Motel in Memphis, the place of Martin Luther King's death, is now the National Civil Rights Museum. It is literally the ground on which his life opened for us the future that is now before us. He saw that the history of African people in America had prepared a covenant for our society. The Promised Land was understood as the inner spiritual agreement that a group had made on behalf of world destiny. It is the power that this group would bring forth to shape the possibilities of culture and to manifest a particular world reality according to their soul development.

The nature of the soul is to manifest reality and the nature of the group soul is to manifest agreements for our shared reality. What W. E. B. Du Bois referred to as the souls of black folks is a collective potential, an inner agreement that can potentially be awakened for the realization of the collective consciousness and the collective striving of a people. Their common initiation legacy gives to the soul qualities and attributes of their ancestral vision through the experience of this great initiation. The soul is initiated and through the soul the human entity creates its personality, its culture, and the age in which we live.

The ending of the twentieth century was prophetically understood as the ending of the color line, an age of governance of race over race, class over class and people over people. It symbolized for people everywhere a call for a distinct freedom not given by civil law but the awakening within the conscious life—how I must be for freedom to be in the world. Inherent in Martin Luther King's work of passive resistance is the capacity to transform the force to fight, to compete, and to oppress someone else's humanity. His work was intended to resist the temptation to take from the other what we are not willing to give to the other. The resistance movement within a violent cultural period was a demonstration of the inner faith of Dr. King's vision. He knew this resistance would strengthen the soul to cross these boundaries of conflict and enter into a world of agreement, the deeper cognitive freedoms that we create within ourselves. He felt that this age was present. He called it a stirring in the world, the troubling of the waters, the power of reconciliation and return.

When I arrived at the National Civil Rights Museum in Memphis and entered the building it resonated with the presence of the ancestors. The ancestral voices echo through the space and interact with the people who come seeking to understand their role in the fulfillment of Martin Luther King's legacy. They enter the spiritual event that remains open through his death. The place serves as a portal of initiation for those who enter with the readiness in their hearts to see the future.

> Well, I don't know what will happen now. We've got some difficult days ahead. But it really doesn't matter with me now, because I've been to the mountaintop. And I don't mind. Like anybody, I would like to live a long life. Longevity has its place. But I'm not concerned about that now. I just want to do God's will. And he's allowed me to go up to the mountain. And I've looked over. And I've seen the Promised Land. I may not get there with you, but I want you to know tonight that we, as a people, will get to the Promised Land. And I'm happy, tonight. I'm not worried about anything. I'm not fearing any man. Mine eyes have seen the glory of the coming of the Lord.

What occurred in this place in 1968 was not just the killing of a man, because what he had taken into his life the night before was a vision of immortality. Immortality is understood as a state of consciousness that extends itself into the future. It is not a biological extension of life but the capacity to envision life beyond one's existence, the power to transcend the given circumstances of life, as well as transcend the contemporary life. It is a function of the soul to awake to its nature beyond the body. Immortals live within the framework of soul consciousness as opposed to body consciousness. In the teachings of Black Gnosticism the African Egyptian mysteries provided initiation for various levels of soul development. Among these processes was a training for what was called the immortals, beings of light, those who live from the soul level illuminating the inner vision to see beyond the veil of the perceptible world. Their intention in this initiatory path was to work with beings of light beyond the temporal space–time continuum and work for something that would be more substantial for what we call reality. Their consciousness by nature was prophetic. They knew what was to come because they had already decided for it.

Dr. King's insights about the vision of immortality give us the aim of his soul work—to work beyond the realms of physical existence for the purpose of fulfilling the inherent truth of the soul of black folks. Upon his death Martin Luther King entered into the prophetic realm where the workings of the ancestral spirits and the workings of the hierarchy in the spiritual world are forging a whole new future. This testimony that he brought forth of the Promised Land brought us closer to the understanding of what this deeper legacy represented as a true and practical potential in the world. This Promised Land is co-created between human beings, ancestors, and the world of spirit. He called us to do our part.

Those who tried to kill him only facilitated the change in his state of presence from physical existence to spiritual existence. The death of someone who had lived so far into the soul that he had awakened the immortal mind is consistent with the Mysteries of Osiris. The dismemberment of the bodies of Osiris did not constitute his death in totality. This initiation into the mysteries of antiquity occurred within the soul. It was not myth. It was a cultural–spiritual practice to initiate humanity into the deeper meanings and possibilities of the worlds of the spirit. The physical death was sometimes necessary for certain spiritual realities to be fulfilled. Dr. King made this known in his statement that "I'm not worried about anything. I'm not fearing any man. Mine eyes have seen the glory of the coming of the Lord."

The power of Isis in the old Memphite tradition was played out again in Memphis, where an initiate places his life before the shrine of immortality, before the love of his people, and promises them a way to freedom without his body but with his faith that we'll get there. From April 4, 1968, until the present time, the work on the Promised Land continues through the sacrifice and awakened conscience of Martin Luther King Jr. Many people have been brought into a great initiation as a result of this one sacrifice. In some ways this is the closing of the circle of what began with the advent of the Middle Passage, the Great Homecoming signaled by his vision of the Promised Land.

As I stood and looked at the place where Martin Luther King died, it became for me a descent into the memory and consciousness of who he is within our tradition. I recall experiencing a movement in my body that felt similar to my experience in the mosque in Burkina Faso. I was going down into a world place where creative forces were shaping destiny and future. I heard King's voice distinctly speaking among many others. I didn't make out clearly what he was saying but my impression was that it concerned a plan that would be made visible to those who are looking for signs.

History is a very peculiar reality in that it belongs completely to the world of the dead. History in our modern sense means looking back at events in time or the human experiences that have informed our present time. But I like to think of history as going down—into the Earth, into the core memory that holds the living legacy of every human being that has come to this Earth, of every human being that has lived in some way for this planet, whether they are known or not. History is the living core memory of the Earth that understands the human place and the human task. Whether we live a long life to accomplish that, or just one day, the Earth takes hold of that memory as an investment in its own future.

There are portals to this Earth memory. Portals whereby we can experience what the Earth has learned about its own evolution from the contribution of human beings. The ground beneath the Lorraine Motel is such a place. It is a place from which we can look, not back at our own struggle and development, but directly into the Earth, and ask, "Are we anywhere closer to understanding this big mystery that called us into this life? And are we willing to take what the Earth is offering in our present time to help us locate where our particular stand can be just as significant as the stand that Martin Luther King took, that has made his life worth remembering?"

We can find such a place on the Earth, we can find such a place in our time. We can be bold enough to take up a cause for perfecting the human process of development and to be able to give to the Earth what it needs to further its own development. The stand we take for the continuity of service to the evolution of our home planet is a contribution to the Earth shrine. It draws from our deeds and our sacrifices a particular energy, an energy that constitutes the life energy of this living planet that is regenerated and redistributed into the elements it unfolds for the ecology that sustains the nature of species. The Earth shrine is our collective archive, our *akashic* record, our ancestral memory, and the transformed substance that our bodies depend on for its continued existence. We live by it because we live within it. It is the law of reciprocity. We reap what we sow. Martin Luther King Jr. tells us:

> It's all right to talk about "long white robes over yonder" in all of its symbolism. But ultimately people want some suits and dresses and shoes to wear down here. It's all right to talk about "streets flowing with milk and honey," but God has commanded us to be concerned about the slums down here and his children who can't eat three square meals a day. It's all right to talk about the New Jerusalem, but one day God's preacher must talk about New York, the new Atlanta, the new Philadelphia, the new Los Angeles, the new Memphis, Tennessee. This is what we have to do.
>
> Now the other thing we have to do is this: Anchor our external direct action with the power of economic withdrawal. Now, we are poor people; individually, we are poor when you compare us with white society in America. We are poor. Never stop and forget that, collectively, that means all of us together; collectively we are richer than all the nations in the world, with the exception of nine. Did you ever think about that? After you leave the United States, Soviet Russia, Great Britain, West Germany, France, and I could name the others, the Negro collectively is richer than most nations of the world. We have an annual income of more than thirty billion dollars a year, which is more than all of the exports of the United States and more than the national budget of Canada. Did you know that? That's power right there, if we know how to pool it.

This stream of humanity that we call Africans had a particular relationship to the Earth and the Earth mysteries, especially those who were brought from West Africa to the Americas. Their knowledge was that the Earth had cycles of time in which it allowed humanity to draw upon particular gifts and use those gifts for cultivating human civilization. They came to America with the knowledge of their own identity, their own culture, and their own place in time.

Culture for the African is not just the framework of how they coexist with each other but how to give back to the Earth to sustain this balance between nature and humanity and more so between the cosmos and humanity. The aim of Black Gnostic tradition is to cultivate practitioners in the discipline of spiritual and social development. The practice is to find the signatures that show up at particular times in world development that signal what must be done for the utilization of the potential that's in the world. We follow these signatures within nature, and within the calendars we keep that structure where we are in the flow of human and spiritual events. The world is not without time and our bodies measure the durations of these messages into our world.

Around fifty years have elapsed from the time of Dr. King's death until where we are now. In this passage of time the inner work on the planes of his spiritual influence has sustained the cultivation of the knowledge of what this inner work would produce outwardly. We were instructed through ceremony and divination during our ritual initiation processes in Africa to observe this fifty-year cycle that corresponds to Dr. King's death. These fifty years in the wilderness, wandering and wondering what had happened to the dream, what had happened to the promise, can now be answered. It was given to our souls. It's in us. We are the dream. The elders teach that prophecy is not a predestined event in and of itself but that human beings are walking in the world as prophecies of what they can create. We live on a threshold between what is and what could be if we decide for it.

Ritual in its sacred context is intended to call forth a prophecy to take what is and place it before the sacred and ask that it be made whole, that it be made more fulfilling, and that it return to us new. This context of adding to what is makes ritual a dynamic and creative aspect of human life and a structure through which prophecies are made manifest. The qualities that we carry within us were cultivated in relationship to our initiation and our contact with the worlds of spirit. This is what we bring to the world through the capacities in our own bodies. We are a continuity of spiritual attributes latent until called forth by the necessities of our time through ritual purpose.

On April 5, 2008, forty years and one day into the making of this covenant of the Promised Land, a ritual was enacted to honor Dr. King's legacy and to inaugurate an institute dedicated to the study and practice of the Black Gnostic tradition, of the prophetic study of history, of what lies within the worlds of the spirit. The ritual was to align with the fortieth year of the revelation of that vision, the conversations with the elder in Burkina Faso to link the shrine there with the place of Martin Luther King's death in Memphis. The Earth shrines in Africa, opened in 2000, supported the opening of other portals in the world. These Earth shrines are generating a renewal and redistribution of the Earth forces for a new human ecology, the making of new covenants.

The portal in Memphis opened by Dr. King's sacrifice was linked to these Earth shrines and particularly the shrine to which I was introduced in Burkina Faso. Our ritual was to activate the shrines in the South of the United States, where the first Africans were enslaved and labored and where they chose to make contact through their spiritual practice with these beings that hosted their future. We knew that April 4th was the signature of the time. We set the intention of the ritual for the inauguration of a study around the prophecy of Martin Luther King's vision specifically in his speech of "I've Been to the Mountaintop" and of his body of work concerning *Agape.*

> Agape is not a weak, passive love. It is love in action. Agape is love seeking to preserve and create community. It is insistence on community even when one seeks to break it. Agape is a willingness to go to any length to restore community. It doesn't stop at the first mile, but it goes the second mile to restore community. It is a willingness to forgive, not seven times, but seventy times seven to restore community. The cross is the eternal expression of the length to which God will go in order to restore broken community. The Resurrection is a symbol of God's triumph over all the forces that seek to block community. The Holy Spirit is the continuing community creating reality that moves through history.

Agape constitutes the making of agreements not only for the making of community but the making of our world to enter into the epigenesis of world potential to balance what we take from nature in right moral measure and intent and what we give to nature as our devoted service toward continuity. It is our willingness to allow our higher faculties of perception and cognition to serve the call of spirit to the levels of an initiation that will further develop the human potential to exist within the love of the future and in service to it.

Agape is the power of the love to open up the Earth shrine, to connect to the collective unconscious of the spiritual streams that runs through the human spiritual social life. We chose the day of April 5, 2008, to open up this covenant between the work that had transpired over the forty years since Dr. King's spiritual ascension and the time frame through which the spiritual architects of this collective soul initiation continued to work its way into our social life.

About 150 people gathered in Los Angeles at the invitation of Shade Tree Multicultural Foundation to inaugurate the World Community Prophecy and Planning Institute. The purpose of the institute is to follow the work of certain cultural avatars including Martin Luther King Jr., W. E. B Du Bois, Langston Hughes, and Pascal Beverly Randolph to open up a deeper understanding of the Mysteries of African peoples in the West. The ritual intention is that the Promised Land will be revealed to the group as a shared understanding of what they can co-create. It is the direct transfer of insight into what the spiritual avatars are willing to give to humanity.

The promise in each of us is to the greater good for others and ourselves. This self-consciousness is the calling forth of the ethics of consciousness to carry for each the task of our collective social aim. The intention is to incarnate into the physical realm the ancestral memory that gives to us the will to expand beingness into the cultural milieu of our time. The dream is the seed that destiny proffers between the spiritual world and the human social world. We create meaningfully when we are aligned with the inner process of this soul agreement.

The ritual that was enacted at the shrine in Burkina Faso in 2001 opened up my understanding to the prophecy of the Promised Land and was also designed to serve in the formulation of strategies for a shared economy. This was not a new endeavor, drawing from African traditional knowledge to form an economic platform for Africans outside of Africa. There have been various attempts to utilize these traditional paradigms in the design of economic platforms. What occurred in the last forty years makes it more probable that our time is right for the use of these shrines, the powers they hold for collective striving and for the alignment of the current resources in our world.

The Earth shrine is where we create our currency. The shrine helps us to create the social picture from the place in which we live. The currencies become the symbolic form of our social spiritual values and our inner word—"that I give to you what I receive from you." It is the acknowledging of the agreement that the human being can ensoul into the physical world spiritual ideals. Currency transmits the human soul forces into a social process and over time builds cultural integrity. It helps develop the person to be able to reach the level of social readiness for deeper possibilities of initiation. When our money systems mature in alignment with the destiny of the members of our society, we allow the spiritual hierarchies and the elemental beings in nature to forge a right ecology of consciousness to support the human spiritual striving.

Different currencies influence human thinking, feeling, and will in various ways. Currencies promote human relationships based on their design and on the mechanisms of their function and flow. They elicit specific behaviors from people and can create social health or social illness based on group practices with that specific form of money. For example, there is a fundamental difference between the United States dollar and the Euro in what their designs are intended to do.

The Euro has a possibility of integrating different cultural expressions into a common economic livelihood without losing the specific cultural significance of each member of the group. It provides a method through which the collective psychology of the group works to mature the local and regional assets and increases participation in their prophetic journey from World War II to present times. The intention of the currency is to bring them out of a historical conflict.

The United States dollar in its design brings the individual to experience optimum self-interest. It has the potential to ideally reach the realm of philanthropy only if those who use this form of money are able to experience and create the free forces necessary to be a giver. Our currency dictates that we must compete in order to achieve our status in society. It does not give full access to initiation as a cultural aim. We learn from this economic model to pursue profit over purpose and materialism over ethical and spiritual development.

Above all most currency systems, including ours, are built on the idea that, in order to be valuable, money must be scarce. Instead of bringing us closer to the understanding of the Earth shrine, scarcity leads us to the dominant trait of violence. The Earth shrine embodies a process that bestows communal wealth, a place to which we dedicate our human will for the working out of the particular disciplines that will support the place in remaining productive and healthy for the right livelihood of human beings and other life beings. In its design people are forced to compete to the extent that many become enemies. Conflict is common in the use of this currency because of the transmission of the value of creating wealth before you create the intention to give.

The Seventh Shrine as a New Practice

The Seventh Shrine, *Imani*, is the human capacity to host the creative process of making something new out of one's own capacity to give and create the necessary meaning for agreement with others. It draws on the human faculty for love and shared understanding to transform the forces that challenge the human experience of living in a world of change. *Imani* or faith prepares us to decide how to contribute to the process of change. Through this human creative gesture of contributing, we acknowledge that the world is not finished. We acknowledge that the human being is the source of reality through which we perceive and understand our unlimited potential of giving. What we call the world is actually accumulated human knowledge of what has been understood, and what we have agreed to is the structure of cognitive frameworks. This allows us to experience our own inner potential and provides for us the means of making contact with the worlds of ideas. This activity takes place within the spheres of the cosmos and with beings in nature and the cosmos that support human development and transformation within the worlds of existence.

Imani is the spiritualization process or the renewing impulse of what we have inherited. It is the inner free force that liberates the human being from the past. *Imani,* or faith, bestows upon us the inner certainty that the world of possibilities that lies before us as prophecy is a common human understanding that we can choose how to use our innate freedoms in a way that hosts the reforming of reality. We have reached a climax in the evolution of our Western journey where the multiple streams of humanity can now meet in a sphere of consciousness above our inherited languages, traditions, and histories through a faculty that has been cultivated by the various forces in the Earth derived from the ancestral sacrifices. These sacrifices now support our spiritual striving for a shared understanding of what the Earth is as a being with gifts. The global impulses that have advanced human cultures now embody a substance—these ancestral sacrifices—that can be experienced through mental and spiritual practices. This gives us a sense of how to renew the agreements that constitute human tradition.

Our understanding of the world, as a global phenomenon, is not humanmade in and of itself. It draws on inner feelings and will, influenced by nature and forces in the cosmos and, fundamentally, it is the underlying unity that is the forces of the Earth. Earth allows us to incarnate the worlds of possibilities into frameworks of agreements through our languages, our arts, and our sciences in order to allow the social, cultural processes to unfold. The indigenous wisdom that defines the Earth as a source of creation and constant change can be witnessed as we look at the current age of humanity, which has found itself at the threshold of radical change. We are to take into consideration the true power and nature of the Earth, not as a source of raw material but as a foundation that allows us to return to the higher worlds of imagination and inspiration. The Earth renews our own covenants for the nature of our beingness. We will see that the Earth supports our capacity to sustain life, the inner life and the outer social life that we share.

Imani brings us to a question: What is the meaning of reality, given our understanding of the transitions that the Earth itself is making? *Imani* points to the initiation of humanity not in our separateness, our own unique histories, bodies, and intentions, but in our wholeness. *Imani* points to the field of probability that if we decide to be the giver of this unique freedom of human consciousness we can support a whole ecology that allows new qualities of life to emerge. When we are exiled from our own inner free disposition of giving, when we are separated from each other through the traditions and prejudices that impose boundaries on our soul's striving, *imani* is a potential harmony out of the conflicts we experience.

It is an invitation into a communion with the self, what knows the unlimited potential and nature of life. It carries within itself the freedom to overcome the oppression of not knowing, the fear of not having, and the doubt of not receiving. *Imani* is the door that we open from the inside to host the guest that brings the inspiration that allows us to re-create the dwelling place to host and to receive abundantly what spirit brings. It is our way of seeing through the eyes of the other the freedoms that we seek. It is community when we are able to live with this Earth as an extension of its own power to sustain life.

Community as Relationship

Community has always been a certain endeavor, an aim, of the human socio-spiritual process, due to our need to be in conversation, and to have a shared reality. If we imagine that the human being brings time into the world, brings eternity into the world, a power that lives beyond sensory perception, beyond the worlds of existence, a power that is genesis itself, a place of beginning, and that must then evolve to become a specific act in the world in relationship to others who are trying to do the same: How do we coordinate eternity to be able to do a common thing when we have such remarkable freedom to be doing what is true for our own inner knowing? So, the process of this spiritual event is that the human being must incarnate into a shared domain of consciousness—one that allows us to mutually acknowledge that we are actually here to do a common task. We are served by the spiritual world to reach our highest potential.

Community allows such a task. The human being moves from the dimension of consciousness of time to consciousness of space, which is relationship. Relationship is that I recognize the mutual intention for a shared understanding of where we must act and when we must act.

Birth allows us to incarnate time. Birth is the point at which the human being moves from eternity into chronology. Birth moves us into a body that creates location of identity. We now begin to organize our spiritual substances and capacities into social impulses.

One of the key acquisitions of this social impulse is language. Language allows us to then communicate the spiritual inner process into a social agreement. A social agreement becomes manifest in the world as civilization, as community. Community can begin to be the domain of a human being within the context of a family, which says, "We are in this framework of love for the relationships that birth has given us in the most intimate context." Or we can begin to look at community from the standpoint of the larger cultural stream into which we are born that has a certain type of tradition. Or we can look at the larger picture of the time in which we were born, the age, the dispensation of which can be an equivalent to about two thousand years of collective memory that shapes what we are working on as a human collective. So, community can be as small as the immediate family, or it can be as large as the age that gives us a collective wisdom of multiple life spans of human endeavors aiming toward a common goal of actualizing a cosmic potential.

Each human being can span both dimensions of time, the local event in the home, or the societal striving to bring into manifestation the workings of cosmic beings, as we hear them in our inner consciousness. Space is a vast territory of memory that allows us to move self, which is intimacy, from an inner place of knowing to an outer act of dedication toward a larger goal that transcends self-interest and puts us in touch with other human beings who are trying to do the same thing, of manifesting the earthly reflection of the heavenly human in us.

The human being cannot live in the isolation of time. Eternity is our own birthright, our spiritual inheritance. As such we have evolved this process of communication to be able to unite with this cosmic power through a language, through word-nature, to have specific types of insight into what could be a collaborative effort in the world. Our speech is a predisposition for agreement. Our speech is a shared awareness that is unique to each human yet common to all. So we strive for a certain understanding of this nature in ourselves and in each other. We can become extremely specific naming what I intend to do with the meaning-giving capacity in my own spiritual potential.

The worldspace is the creative endeavor of human beings that are creating out of nothing, creating—out of spiritual substance or "thought" and meaning—a genuine type of artifact that we call reality. It allows us to develop a consciousness that reflects beauty, goodness, truth, and love for a future that is not yet created. Community can only be co-created. It's attained when we dream into each others' lives, giving from ourselves what we do best and freely allowing the others to receive from such gifts. It's created as a grace when we live out who we truly are. The purpose of our life becomes revealed through the flow of time.

When we communicate a worldspace is formed supporting what can be probable out of the realms of possibility. A worldspace is a unity due to its being structured by our understanding of what will be manifested. What we create and bring into manifestation is a result of our understanding. This can be shared. So we can look at the world of our creative activity and say, "It's good." It allows us to continue to feel united in that common truth. Agreement is the foundation stone for sustainable reality.

If we're not communicating, we create the forces that separate us. It is our communication that unites us. The individual human being—a source of freedom to be oneself in relationship to the other being in community—does not take away the individuality. On the contrary it strengthens even more the individual's path and the continuity of the shared awareness in relationship to others.

We can find all over the world, all through the ages of our time, that freedom has been always with us. It has become compounded in our modem reality because of the social practices. Particularly the practice of our economy that puts before us an incentive to seek self-interest, to profit above the common good, to compete for a place in the world—when in fact we could cooperate and produce more of what we compete for. We have models of social life that put this type of incentive before the human being at a time when we have not yet been able to develop a self-awareness that represents a shared reality. People then begin to pursue not individuation, not the psychological and spiritual development of their own capacity to give. Individualism is the practice of not participating in the collective good. Individualism is seeking self-interest, because it allows people to feel secure in ownership, which they think brings future money.

So we have this self-interest in our midst, and it's taking hold of the human will power more and more. It's not the only thing—there are also religious–spiritual systems that give us the idea that salvation is a personal goal, and that you can arrive somewhere and leave others behind. So we have this compounding as well the inner spiritual aspiration of people, this idea that love is for being outside of time, outside of place, that we can in a sense arrive at that relationship without having to share any social responsibility for love on the Earth.

Then we have a scientific model that tells us we are born out of biological necessity, and if we're able to meet the hierarchy of needs in a biological way, then we are in a sense at the peak of our rise to life and the "survival of the fittest" of those who are able to meet those needs.

We're in a type of civilization that makes it hard to pursue community. The currency system that we work through in our economic life tells us that the resources that we have to live with must be scarce in order to be valuable. So we can't share or else we will undermine our own survival.

I think it's possible for human beings to take a certain type of exploration of building confidence through the faculties of love and shared meaning to resolve those types of gaps in the social process that we share. I think it will allow us to rediscover that the true nature and true inheritance of the human being—let's say the "predisposition"—is to retain all of those things in the interest of a shared life. We can draw from the experience of nature that nature creates in abundance. We can draw from the cosmic law within the human being that we create out of nothing. That is the nature of the human being.

The human being has always lived in a complex world reality. Even in primitive ages, there was still a certain complexity; we just don't know about it. We have now moved into an age of knowledge whereby we know how complex reality is.

We know particularly the level of complexity we've reached is that we have arrived at a place where we say—and this is the dilemma—that everyone has a right to their opinion of what reality is, what we call the subjective worldview. So you share something about your understanding of reality, and someone will say, "Well, that's your opinion." Even though we still try to communicate something that we want to share, to have a shared understanding.

This struggle to bridge the gap is not just between locations of culture—North America or Europe or Africa or Asia, these domains of human collectives that have to do with geographical distance. What is a challenge for us is being able to arrive at a place above the given language barriers, the given economic barriers, the given social barriers that we have decided are boundaries in and of themselves for human beings and our experiences.

Over time, we've created more countries than were in the world before. We've made it such that people have created very specific class domains to decide social necessities, social needs. This is where the complexity is occurring—in our tendency to name distinctions, to the degree that we create more and more exclusive places of culture. We feel we have a right to be separate from the masses of people.

The technology that allows us to get from Johannesburg, South Africa, to South Central, Los Angeles, is easier now. But the motive is more complex. Why are we going? For a lot of people, migration is for economic incentives. Or, to a certain degree we migrate even more now for safety. In some areas of the world, one runs a risk of being persecuted by staying put.

We thought it might be that because we are in the "modern world" it would be best. We've created more refugees now in the twenty-first century than we've had before. We've elevated through technology what we call "weapons of mass destruction," to the degree that people have to abandon locations of culture and home, becoming refugees in search of sanctuary and another form of community that will allow them to live in the world.

Bridging the gaps has to do more with working through the subjective views of what we call reality, where some feel they have the exclusive right to decide how social groups should be. If we take what's going on in Iraq, or any other place where there's a certain conflict, and we look behind the insanity of what's going on there—we say it's "democracy," "helping people establish democracy." There is just the appearance of a social system to vote. There is not real shared understanding or shared agreement of what that vote means for the future. It is naive realism.

What we should support is the distribution of the incentive for people to participate in communities that reflect back to them the predisposition of the human being. We should support communities that reflect human life, what we actually strive to establish, the right to movement, even the right to love. What I think is still trying to be preserved is the self-interest that is dominating global culture. If people love, the institutions of our age will dissolve. There are people who are very seriously invested in the status quo of civilization, where in order to remain in power, people must be separated and governed by the fragmentation that exists.

Freedom of movement begins with us re-imagining how to host a guest, understanding that there are people who need to be where we are in order for a new type of conversation to become. We have no exclusive right to enforce the boundaries on the human beings we call "countries." We have no right to enforce policies that limit people's access to land, water, and movement.

This is the fundamental experience of the spirit—the spirit is movement on a basic level. What the human being searches for is a framework that, through conversation, can allow agreements of shared participation in cultivating the resources of the Earth to enter into home life, communal life, and eventually civilization.

We practice a life process of limiting our movement. The global age requires more participation in the flow of resources, including people, allowing people to meet. We see that it is very common whereby people have arrived from different parts of the Earth, sharing their stories of self-development—people sharing what's happening elsewhere in the world, and incentives toward global participation. I think that will become more common. I think we need to prepare to host people who are searching for this, who have this common good that they share.

Participation is essential to the forming and the sustaining of community. If we take just the word "part," it points only to the individual human being. But we must create this other aspect of "participation," which is reciprocity, the exchange of the common good. This is the nature of community, a process of exchanging with each other and cultivating something that I can't create by myself. I can't create something that complex by myself. It is a discovery that when we participate, the emergent quality is something that spontaneously reveals itself, that in the act of hosting and being hosted in this improvisation of devotion to some aspect of our human genius, we arrive at something that we couldn't see beforehand. You could say that we share this "communion," this wonderful substance. This is the "precipitation" of the spiritual substance of human life. It condenses, it manifests, and it becomes now tangible in the world. Participation is rain in the world. It's *manna* in the world. It is the incarnation of the future in the world. The parts by themselves have it as a potential. When we come together we create the bonds that allow it to become a substance that the individual part cannot create alone.

African slavery in America paid forward an economy. It was not just that they worked without compensation. They worked to be compensated from a level of soul to create a type of seeing that allowed the veil that obscures the prophetic vision to be transformed. Their spiritual economy emerges from what Du Bois called the Second Sight or what the African Gnostic tradition speaks of as divine seership. Their initiation cultivates an economy from slavery to philanthropy, the transforming of the moral intention to be a giver through forced labor: Harmony through Conflict.

The wealth that is spoken of here is human wealth created through the initiation of consciousness from one state to another, creation of capacity within the soul, that allows the human being to experience higher cognitive states of awareness. These higher states represent principles of inner self-consciousness and the practical world formulation and strategic frameworks, which through agreement become social thought and practice. This leads to the creation of a social Will for the development of human society. It is a transformation of the world through the initiation of the human being.

Initiation releases into the personality of the individual capacities for the development of character and destiny. It prepares and puts the human being in contact with entities both human and divine. Through these particular fields of relatedness, consciousness is developed. Through these primal intuitions that become available with expanding spiritual awareness, new resources are discovered and created. This is the core of human wealth, the opening of consciousness to the higher expression of soul–spiritual capacity. All sciences and arts that shape human society are sourced by this human experience. It can be called forth through the personal practice of contemplation on one's inner life experience. It becomes more active when we cultivate the relationship that allows us to utilize these latent capacities. Relationship generates for us the worldspace for the creation of culture and what we call civilization.

The term *value* serves to guide the human being toward collective consciousness. These qualities within the feeling life and the moral social awareness of people give rise to a particular orientation to the communities that they will form. Values are often the catalyst for the agreements that people make for the social tasks that they engage. They serve to inspire, promote, and at times protect the particular human social interests for the fulfillment of group destiny. Values in and of themselves are not the end of the human process of development. They help prepare the human being to meet the task of the time.

Values, before they are social, are psychological. They remain in the human consciousness as a search for meaning. When we, as human beings, find ourselves on this search for meaning through the values that we attend to, we elevate our initiation experience to the level of the social. It is here that agreements must now be made, not just to reinforce the values that have brought us to this point of encounter but to work on understanding what lies beyond this threshold. Values must be changed for the human being to change and for society to change.

Agreement is an inner process that begins with the decision within the human being to go beyond what is known within our own state of consciousness and through experiencing the paradigm of the other to create an understanding. This understanding within the person brings them to another level of conscious awareness where the conversation moves from the boundaries of conflict into the flow of mutual consent for another level of creativity that we call a covenant. A covenant is a state of consciousness that allows human beings to work on their future without confining themselves to the values of their time. We must work this way in order to create a new knowledge that is not yet visible in our cultural space. The covenant helps us to work from the future with the free spiritual forces of the future toward our present time. It is only an inner law of love for something that is not yet in existence that allows the human being to initiate the act of creating covenants.

Agreements happen with the framework of the individual and communal life. A covenant lies within reach of human beings, not in relationship to the place where they exist, but the time in which they exist. When a covenant is to be called forth we act out of the impulse of what the time requires of us. For example, our current age presents us with the challenge of global warming. This occurs not in relationship to a particular place but something that calculates for us the variables of what we call time, which is the inner consciousness awareness of what "I" must do and be in order for reality to be different. This dilemma puts before human beings a threshold for the evolution of consciousness. Either we change without figuring out many details and allow that future to bring us into itself or we experience the dilemma that initiation will bring. A covenant helps us to act on faith toward this future event where what comes after us brings us life. This is for the benefit of the world and the future.

Slavery for the particular group of people who emerged out of an ancestral memory provided a shared context into which this memory was given. The ancestral memory that Africans brought supported their economic life in their historical cultural belongings, their places of origin. Their consciousness supported reality above and beyond their enslavement. They utilized this power of thought conception and the power of will to practice the creation of a covenant among themselves for a time different from when they were enslaved. They utilized the spirit of reality we call night that had, for Africans, the understanding of the world of the spirit. This world of spirit is where the forces of night that allow human beings to dream and to become aware of the higher forces of destiny—what we call the stars—guide the human soul to future states of consciousness. The Africans' love for this future generated a movement of energies from one time frame to another. They imagined their descendants free. They prepared within their soul a legacy to be passed on and to be supported by the time spirit, the ancestral spirit that they had made contact with. These entities are spiritual allies that now guide the human being to the right time, place, and event for the awakening of this soul memory that is their inheritance to become self-conscious.

It is the homecoming of their ancestral gift when people are able to enter the agreement that they are not without an inheritance. The soul holds within itself that spiritual stream, into which a person is born, the occult powers that, through divination, can be fully understood and utilized for the creation of specific reality. It is through the activity of our mind—the utilization of mental, psychical, and moral disciplines—that the human being becomes oriented to a state of consciousness we call future, the freedom from the past.